Globaliz

Globalization and the Welfare State

Ramesh Mishra

Professor Emeritus of Social Policy, York University, Canada

Edward Elgar
Cheltenham, UK • Northampton, MA, USA

Published by
Edward Elgar Publishing Limited
Glensanda House
Montpellier Parade
Cheltenham
Glos GL50 1UA
UK

Edward Elgar Publishing, Inc.
136 West Street
Suite 202
Northampton
Massachusetts 01060
USA

A catalogue record for this book
is available from the British Library

Library of Congress Cataloguing in Publication Data
Mishra, Ramesh, Dr.
     Globalization and the welfare state / Ramesh Mishra.
     1. Social policy.   2. Welfare state.   3. International economic
relations.   I. Title.
HN17.5.M565   1999
361.6'5—dc21   99–21912
                                                                        CIP

ISBN 1 85898 221 9 (cased)
        1 84064 173 8 (paperback)

Typeset by Manton Typesetters, 5–7 Eastfield Road, Louth, Lincs, LN11 7AJ, UK.
Printed in the United Kingdom at the University Press, Cambridge

Contents

List of Figures and Tables   vi
List of Abbreviations   vii
Acknowledgements   viii
Introduction   ix

1   The logic of globalization: the changing context of the welfare
    state   1
2   Employment, labour market and income: growing insecurity and
    inequality   18
3   Social policy in retreat or the hollowing out of the welfare state 36
4   Social policy and democracy: do politics still matter?   53
5   Globalization in comparative perspective: Sweden, Germany and
    Japan   74
6   The logic of globalization revisited   94
7   Towards a global social policy   111

References   133
Index   147

Figures and Tables

Figure 7.1   Global actors and social policy   123

Table 3.1   Top central government marginal personal tax rates (%)
            on earnings (selected OECD countries)   42
Table 3.2   Overall (national and local) corporate tax rates (%)
            (selected OECD countries)   43

List of Abbreviations

AFDC	Aid to Families with Dependent Children
CSJ	Commission on Social Justice (UK)
EC	European Community
EMU	European monetary union
EU	European Union
G7	Group of Seven (Industrialized Nations)
GATT	General Agreement on Tariffs and Trade
GDP	Gross Domestic Product
ICESCR	International Covenant on Economic Social and Cultural Rights (UN)
IGO	Intergovernmental organization
ILO	International Labour Organization
IMF	International Monetary Fund
INGO	International non-governmental organization
ISM	International social movement
KWS	Keynesian welfare state
MAI	Multilateral Agreement on Investment
MNCs	Multinational corporations
NAFTA	North American Free Trade Agreement
NGO	Non-governmental organization
OECD	Organization for Economic Co-operation and Development
OPEC	Organization of Petroleum-Exporting Countries
UN	United Nations
WB	World Bank
WTO	World Trade Organization

Acknowledgements

Colleagues who were generous with their time and shared their ideas on globalization and social policy with me include Daniel Drache, Karl Hinrichs, Alfred Kahn, Sheila Kamerman, Stephan Leibfried, Claus Offe, Frances Fox Piven, Martin Seeleib-Kaiser, Theda Skocpol and Michael Zuern.

Professors Daniel Drache and Patricia Evans, colleagues at York University, read the entire book in its draft stage. I am grateful for their comments and suggestions, only some of which I have been able to take into account. Dr Priscilla Harding, my former student, acted as research assistant for a time and later as reader and editor of the book. I am grateful for her valuable assistance.

The Institute for Fiscal Studies kindly granted permission to reproduce figures from J. Owens 'Globalization: The Implications for Tax Policies', *Fiscal Studies* 14 (3), 1993. An earlier version of chapter 7 of this book appeared as 'Beyond the Nation State: Social Policy in an Age of Globalization' in *Social Policy and Administration* 32 (5), 1998 and later as a chapter in C. J. Finer (ed.) *Transnational Social Policy*, Oxford and Malden, Mass., Blackwell, 1999. Finally, thanks are due to the Social Sciences and Humanities Research Council of Canada for providing me with a grant which made the research for this book possible.

Introduction

Globalization has spawned a vast literature, very little of which is about its impact on the welfare state. This book explores this multifaceted impact. Its focus is on economic globalization, understood as the openness of national economies with respect to trade and financial flows but seen very much in political and ideological terms. A major theme of the book is that economic globalization has been shaped essentially by the politics and ideology of neoliberalism, so that it could almost be characterized as neoliberalism writ large.

What accounts for the astonishing élan and verve of a free market utopia seeking to further its hegemony throughout the world? The book argues that the collapse of communism and the absence of any systemic alternative to a market economy are what is fuelling this ideology. The book therefore begins by sketching the political correlates of economic globalization, namely the collapse of communism and the retreat of democratic socialism as a credible alternative.

As far as the welfare state is concerned globalization raises two main issues. First, does economic openness deprive nation states of their policy autonomy – the ability to shape social policy – and if so, what are the implications for systems of social protection? Secondly, does globalization entail a downward spiralling of social standards – a race to the bottom – as nations vie with one another to compete in the international market place?

The book argues that the opening up of economies has curtailed the policy autonomy of nation states in the area of macroeconomic management for full employment and economic growth. Moreover pressures – in part political and ideological – stemming from globalization have impinged significantly on labour markets, taxation, social spending and systems of social protection. And the arrow points downward.

Globalization has also undermined the first line of defence against poverty and dependence of the Keynesian welfare state, namely full employment and well-paid full-time jobs (primarily for males, admittedly). Greater openness and competition have given capital an important lever to 'flexibilize' labour markets and depress wages. The second line of defence against poverty and dependency, namely systems of social protection, has weakened less, mainly because of electoral democracy. Thus the population of industrialized nations

continues to enjoy a broad measure of social security, although income inequality has increased – sharply in some countries – and the tax burden for
social programmes has shifted downward. These changes are far more in
evidence in Anglo-Saxon countries from which most of the data for this book
are drawn.

The comparative evidence presented in this book suggests that in Continental Europe and Japan income inequality has increased a good deal less
and institutions of social protection remain far more intact compared with
Anglo-Saxon countries. Indeed the evidence suggests that there is more than
one route to flexibility and competitiveness and that globalization, led by the
US, is privileging the neoliberal route of extensive deregulation and minimal
social protection.

Welfare states also need to be seen as forming a part of the broader
configuration of institutions and practices embodied in the three models of
capitalism, namely the Anglo-Saxon (US), the West European (Germany) and
the East Asian (Japanese). Moreover the two latter models have strong inbuilt
elements of a social market approach with considerable systemic resistance
to a move in the direction of Anglo-Saxon capitalism.

Nevertheless neoliberal politics and ideology threaten to become hegemonic
influences on globalization – as evidenced by the OECD and IMF's persistent
advocacy for the neoliberal brand of 'flexibility' and 'competitiveness'. These
and other IGOs, largely under the sway of right-wing economic orthodoxy
and American influence, are playing a considerable role in furthering globalization. After reviewing the comparative evidence the book therefore concludes
that, as globalization continues to push ahead in its present neoliberal path,
pressures on West European and Japanese social market models to deregulate
and to lower social standards will intensify.

In the final chapter therefore the book calls for a transnational social policy
for protection of social standards. Essentially it amounts to confronting 'globalization from above' with 'globalization from below', or put differently,
countering 'globalization from the Right' with 'globalization from the Left'.
The proposals presented in the final chapter along these lines are rather
general and much more work is needed to make a transnational approach to
social policy a viable project. The political problems that such a project will
encounter are also formidable. Hence the final chapter includes a brief review
of the modest progress to date of UN agencies which, along with a growing
body of INGOs, represent globalization from 'the other side'.

Global sceptics will have nothing to do with *international* action in defence of social standards since they believe that globalization is largely a
myth and that national governments are reasonably free to set their own
policies. At the other extreme are those who maintain that nothing short of
the renationalization of economies, complete with capital controls and other

forms of regulation, can restore a nation's policy autonomy and ability to protect social standards. Others argue that the struggle against neoliberalism and globalization must be waged squarely on *national* terrain and not in the nebulous arena of international action.

This book is based on the belief that a social response to globalization needs to be made both at the national *and* at the transnational level. Moreover, the supranational level of decision-making connected with regional associations such as the EU and NAFTA as well as with global institutions such as the IMF, the WB and WTO, is of growing importance. In this sense globalization could be seen as presenting welfare state theory and practice with the challenge – and also the opportunity – to match economic globalization with social globalization. That is the concluding, and prescriptive, argument of this book.

The book is organized as follows. Chapter 1 considers the nature and meaning of globalization and outlines its impact on the welfare state in the form of a set of propositions which articulate the 'logic' of globalization. Chapter 2 looks at employment and the labour market in a globalizing economy. Chapter 3 considers the direct and indirect consequences of economic openness for systems of social protection and taxation. Chapter 4 reviews the prospect of democratic opposition within the nation state to globalization pressures. Chapter 5 examines the evidence from Sweden, Germany and Japan on internationalization and social protection to complement the evidence presented earlier largely from Anglo-Saxon countries. Chapter 6 considers the validity of the 'logic' of globalization thesis in light of preceding arguments and evidence. Finally, Chapter 7 calls for a transnational approach to social policy and social standards.

1. The logic of globalization: the changing context of the welfare state

Three major developments in recent decades have altered the economic, political and ideological context of the welfare state in important ways. They are: the collapse of the socialist alternative, the globalization of the economy, and the relative decline of the nation state. Although overlapping and interrelated, each of these has implications for the welfare state which require us to reconsider some of the basic ideas and assumptions which have guided thinking about social policy and social welfare since the Second World War (WW2). And although the focus of our inquiry is globalization – largely as an economic phenomenon – we wish to avoid the economism implicit in the concept from the outset. As we shall argue later, globalization is an economic phenomenon driven by politics and ideology. We therefore begin with the political developments of the late 20th century.

THE COLLAPSE OF THE SOCIALIST ALTERNATIVE

Arguably the most dramatic and unanticipated event of the late 20th century is the collapse of communism as a social system. At the very least it implies the end of the Marxist–Leninist version of socialism. Less dramatic but also significant is the waning of the prospect of a parliamentary transition to socialism in the West. In short, at least for the *foreseeable future* – let us put it no more strongly than that – the prospect of a viable and progressive systemic alternative to capitalism seems to have disappeared. This is an unprecedented situation since virtually the beginning of industrial capitalism in the 19th century. Indeed one might say that the system of social protection which became institutionalized as a set of social rights after WW2 grew up in the shadow of socialism. Since the days of Bismarck the socialist vision and ideology inscribed on the banner of the labour movement acted as a spur to social reform. Put simply, the threat to private ownership of the means of production and property more generally presented by socialism and the labour movement compelled the compromise – the relative decommodification – of certain of the life-chances of capitalist society. Indeed beginning in the 1880s the socialist movement and socialist

1

ideas – broadly conceived – made a spectacular advance for nearly a century (Therborn, 1984).

The Bolshevik revolution and the birth of the USSR signalled the emergence of a new society. The economic and political crisis of Western capitalism during the interwar years, culminating in the Great Depression, mass unemployment and a hugely destructive world war, made it a social order very much on the defensive. The acceptance, in broad outlines, by the parties of the Right of the full employment welfare state was the result, among other things, of the growing strength of the Left alternative. Both the Marxist and non-Marxist Left made significant advances in the early post-WW2 decades (Therborn). Moreover, a socialist world had come into existence which challenged morally and materially, at least in the early post-war decades, the social system of capitalism. Full employment, social security and collective consumption formed an integral part of the more developed of these societies, an aspect of socialist society that the general population seems to have admired most (Mishra, 1977, p. 147).

Until the 1970s an evolutionary as well as a revolutionary road to socialism seemed a real possibility in the West. The presence of a socialist world outside and a socialist labour opposition within made the inequities and insecurities of a market society hard to justify. It was the potential threat of system transformation that gave rise to the legitimation problem addressed by the welfare state (O'Connor, 1973; Habermas, 1976). Moreover, the full employment welfare state came to be seen as the accommodation of a market society to collectivist values and aspirations – a 'middle way' between laissez-faire capitalism on the one hand and state socialism on the other. True, the explosive growth of social expenditure and the general acceptance of the welfare state in the early post-WW2 decades was the result of a host of factors. Nonetheless the possibility of an alternative society which could conceivably replace liberal capitalism provided the broad ideological context for making assessment about politically tolerable levels of unemployment, inequality and other issues.

As the 1980s wore on, the prospect of socialism began to look increasingly remote. The disarray of Keynesianism in the 1970s was followed by a flurry of industrial militancy giving rise to problems of 'governance', but did not result in a challenge to the capitalist social order. Rather, politics in the West, especially in English-speaking countries, took a right turn with the resurgence of the ideas of neoliberalism.

For a time it looked as though Eurocommunism and Swedish-style social democracy might provide a way forward for the Left, leading to a parliamentary transition to socialism (Mishra, 1984, Chapters 3 and 4, *passim*). With the subsequent collapse of communism and the retreat of parliamentary socialism in Sweden, the socialist alternative has virtually disappeared. The collapse of the socialist alternative and the disappearance of any serious internal threat from the labour movement has made possible the return of classical capitalism with its ideal of a free market economy and the drive towards deregulation and privatization.

Clearly with no rival in sight and as the only system capable of delivering economic growth and the cornucopia of consumer goods, capitalism has become almost self-legitimating (Mishra, 1996). In so far as the system no longer faces a legitimation problem (except perhaps connected with the environment) the incentive for attending to problems of social justice has weakened substantially. Not surprisingly a higher level of insecurity, poverty and inequality has become acceptable in many countries with no untoward political consequences. The retreat from the mixed economy and the welfare state is visible everywhere with the Anglo-Saxon countries leading the way.

True, the radical potential of organized labour and the prospect of a socialist alternative were only a part of the complex web of causation of the welfare state. Moreover as Pierson's (1994) admirable study demonstrates, the factors that are preventing the retrenchment of the welfare state are not necessarily those that brought it into being in the first place. Thus electoral competition, the popularity of social programmes, the influence of interest groups and other vested interests spawned by social programmes themselves – these and other aspects of liberal democracy constitute a formidable resistance to welfare state retrenchment. True, these and other countervailing influences have been at work and it is largely due to these that so far even under regimes with a strong ideological commitment to rolling back state welfare, the erosion of social rights has been limited. Such considerations have led to the belief that the welfare state is here to stay, that it has become almost 'irreversible' (Mishra, 1990; Pierson, 1994).

It is the thesis of this book that globalization has introduced a new element into the situation, weakening very considerably the influence of domestic national politics on social policy. The emergence of a global market economy and the need for global competitiveness have handed neoliberalism a powerful new weapon with which to contain and neutralize the counter-pressure of domestic politics. The sweep and ascendancy of a global market economy has, of course, as its corollary the collapse of communism and the retreat of the socialist alternative more generally. This is the essential context of today's globalization.

GLOBALIZING THE ECONOMY

Globalization refers to a process through which national economies are becoming more open and thus more subject to supranational economic influences and less amenable to national control. However the precise nature and extent of globalization remains a matter of debate and contention.[1] A useful distinction is that between the *internationalization* of economies and *globalization* proper (Hirst and Thompson, 1996, pp. 8–13; Petrella, 1996). In the former case the principal economic units remain national although international aspects of the economy, e.g. trade, foreign direct investment and multinational enterprises, assume increasing importance. Despite the greater openness of economies, however, international economic activity can be seen largely as an extension of the national. For example MNCs retain a clear national base and are amenable to regulation by the mother country.

Globalization proper, on the other hand, refers to a situation where distinct national economies cease to exist in that they are subsumed and rearticulated into the system by international processes and transactions (Hirst and Thompson, 1996, p. 10). Production becomes truly global as transnational corporations without national identity, truly footloose and with international management, replace MNCs. Corporations become 'stateless' and national governments can no longer regulate or control these global corporations. The international economic system becomes autonomous and can be regulated only at the international level (ibid., pp. 10–11).

The distinction between the two is important, argue Hirst and Thompson, in the sense that the degree of internationalization of economies has varied historically and today's relatively greater openness of economies is not a new phenomenon. It can therefore be seen as conjunctural or cyclical and thus reversible. On the other hand the globalization of economies in the sense defined above would be an unprecedented development in world history, a truly structural transformation of the world economy with major implications for the autonomy of the nation state. Careful examination of the data suggests that what we have today is more akin to greater internationalization than globalization (Hirst and Thompson, 1996; Wade, 1996, p. 61). However, most analysts seem to agree that these two must be seen as ideal types, not necessarily mutually exclusive. Thus a development towards globalization remains possible, although evidence suggests that what we have today is an international rather than a global economy. In this book the term globalization will be used in an inclusive sense, i.e. to denote both the internationalization as well as transnationalization of economies unless the context requires that a clear distinction be made between the two.

As mentioned already, global sceptics such as Hirst and Thompson argue that the internationalization of economies is nothing new. Trade liberalization, the growing importance of imports and exports in a nation's economy, increasing foreign direct investment and the like have been a feature of the post-WW2 economy of Western countries although they have also grown in importance for domestic economies (Hirst and Thompson, 1996, pp. 261–

31). Moreover, the economies of some of the leading welfare states, e.g. Sweden and Germany, have had a great deal of openness, in the sense of trade dependence, for a long time (Esping-Andersen, 1996c, p. 257; Garrett, 1998, pp. 57–8).

However the most dramatic and significant change from the viewpoint of the welfare state is that of financial globalization, i.e. money and capital have been set free to move across national boundaries. True, as global sceptics point out this too is not a new development. Before WW1 Britain and a number of other countries were more open in terms of capital movement and the role of foreign trade in their economies (Hirst and Thompson, 1996, pp. 27–8). However, *from the standpoint of the welfare state* the financial openness of economies is an entirely new and significant development. The point is that before 1914 when economies were more open, there was no welfare state – no Keynesian macroeconomic management to maintain full employment, no universal social programmes and no high levels of taxation. Conversely, after WW2 when modern welfare states came into being, Western economies were relatively closed and self-contained.

It is this structural dependence of the welfare state on a relatively closed economy that is the crucial issue. More particularly, until the 1970s all Western countries had strict control over capital movement and exchange rates were fixed. These arrangements were a part of the post-war reconstruction of the international economy under the Bretton Woods agreement. The United States acted as the lynchpin of the system through a convertible dollar.

The American decision in 1971 to end convertibility dealt a body blow to the Bretton Woods system. In 1974 the United States abolished capital controls. Britain followed in 1979. By then Keynesian demand management was in disarray and neoliberal economics was in ascendancy. By the early 1990s most OECD nations had dismantled capital controls (Kelly, 1995, p. 216; Helleiner, 1996, p. 193). Exchange rates had long ceased to be fixed. Financial globalization had made giant strides. Money and capital were free to move across countries and businesses were free to invest world-wide. Thanks to the development of microelectronics and computers, huge sums of money could be moved around the globe within seconds. Meanwhile MNCs and their share in world trade had grown steadily (Wade, 1996, pp. 61–6). Taken together, these developments have changed the context in which welfare states operated during the golden age of welfare capitalism.

One major consequence of the changes outlined above is that the autonomy of national governments to manage their economies so as to ensure full employment and economic growth has been curtailed. Keynesian macroeconomic management, e.g. generating employment and economic growth through reflationary policies, presupposes a relatively closed national economy which can be regulated by the national government. 'Reflation in one country' is not a feasible option in an open economy. As the Socialist Government in France, for example, discovered in 1981, instead of boosting domestic production and creating jobs, economic stimuli boosted imports, resulting in balance of payments problems and a seriously weakened currency. The Government had to abandon its reflationary policy (Hall, 1987).

Full employment can no longer be achieved through demand management by a single country in an open economy. The same openness makes it difficult for nations to pursue a monetary policy, e.g. one of low interest rates, independently of other nations especially large trend-setting economies such as the United States. In principle, although to a lesser extent in practice so far, the same is true of fiscal policy. High rates of taxation on corporate profits and higher incomes risk driving capital to more 'investor-friendly' countries, thus reducing employment and investment. The same applies, in principle at any rate, to regulatory and industrial relations policies which are perceived as unfavourable to business. Thus in Sweden when capital controls were removed in the mid-1980s there was virtually a haemorrhage of capital out of the country (Pontusson, 1992, pp. 332–3). Put simply, by providing capital with an 'exit' option, globalization has strengthened the bargaining power of capital very considerably against government as well as labour.

Indeed in so far as this is true, this above all is what is 'new' about globalization from the viewpoint of the politics of the welfare state. It is not the economic facts about globalization as such but their *political* implications that make this a new and significant phenomenon. Thus money and investment capital can vote with their feet if they do not like government policies. The threat of relocation or refusal to invest at home may be enough to get concessions from the work-force on wages and working conditions.

The end of full employment has also weakened the leverage of organized labour. Employers do not need the co-operation of unions to achieve wage moderation, flexibility and changes in workplace practices. Unemployment, monetarism and the increasing deregulation of labour markets suffice to keep wages and prices down and to secure worker compliance with management needs. As a result tripartism and a consensual approach to economic management have suffered a decline as market relations give more power to capital (see pp. 59–60).

The upshot of all this is to undermine the post-war social democratic strategy of managing national economies through Keynesian and neocorporatist means. Indeed globalization virtually sounds the death-knell of the classical social democratic strategy of full employment, high levels of public expenditure and progressive taxation (Teeple, 1995).[2] With social democracy bereft of its arsenal of policies, nation states are deprived of viable alternatives to neoliberal and monetarist policies. Increasingly the parties of the Left and

Centre are being reduced to following policies that differ only in degree from those of their opponents on the Right (see pp. 54–6).

Finally, given the openness of economies and the increasing importance of trade, international competitiveness is at a premium. True, the degree of trade dependence of economies as well as the meaning of 'international competitiveness' remain controversial issues. Moreover, there is not necessarily a single route to competitiveness. However the well-known, neoliberal route to cost-competitiveness and profitability is through 'social dumping', i.e. moving or threatening to move operations to locations with lower wages and working conditions, less social protection and regulation and lower taxes. At any rate globalization enhances the prospect for social dumping, i.e. a downward spiral in wages, working conditions and social expenditures, as countries vie with each other to compete in the global market place and to make conditions more 'investor-friendly'.

The argument so far has been presented in the form of the 'logic' of globalization, namely, given the nature of economic changes involved in globalization what might be the logical consequences as far as full employment and social protection are concerned? Although prima facie evidence lends plausibility to this argument, the extent to which the real world corresponds to its deductive logic is a matter that we will consider in later chapters.

Suffice to say at this point, however, that the impact of globalization seems to vary from one part of the world to another. Thus it is in the Anglo-Saxon countries that the trends and tendencies outlined above seem to be most clearly in evidence. Continental Europe has travelled much less far down the road of deregulating labour markets, reducing social benefits and expenditures and lowering taxes. The same could be said about Japan, whose system of social protection, however, differs in important ways from that of the West as indeed does Japanese society as a whole.

The similarity between the logic of globalization and neoliberal economics and in turn the association of these two with policies of Anglo-Saxon countries raises the question of the relationship between neoliberalism and globalization (Piven, 1995). In this connection an important point to note is that globalization is not simply a market-driven economic phenomenon. It is also – and very much – a political and ideological phenomenon. Once this is understood then the debate about the exact nature and extent of globalization as an 'objective' economic phenomenon and the apparent paradox of national states furthering globalization appear in a new light.[3] Thus globalization must also be understood as the transnational ideology of neoliberalism which seeks to establish its ascendancy world-wide. Not surprisingly this ideology has its source and inspiration in the Anglo-Saxon world – the spiritual home of neoliberalism – and more particularly in Anglo-American capitalism.

Albert (1993), Hutton (1995a) and others have sought to demonstrate that there are several varieties of capitalism in the world today. Within the Occident there is at least a European or 'Rhine' model of capitalism typified by Germany and a neoliberal form of capitalism represented by the United States. Whereas systems of social protection and social consensus are integral components of the social market capitalism of Western Europe, neoliberal capitalism espouses a free market ideology with a minimum of social protection. Globalization is a process that is helping to extend and consolidate the hegemony of the latter form of capitalism world-wide. Intergovernmental organizations such as the meetings of G7 countries, the IMF, OECD, the WB and the WTO are playing a major part in this process (Clarke and Barlow, 1997; Brecher and Costello, 1994; Korten, 1995, pp. 173–81). Directly or indirectly they are involved in promoting the deregulation, commodification and privatization of economic activities as well as in downsizing government and scaling down social protection.

Since the late 1970s the IMF and WB have been imposing austerity policies on Third World countries in the form of structural adjustment programmes and other changes as a condition for the granting or rescheduling of loans (Deacon et al., 1997, pp. 61–2; Ghai, 1991). Currently the former communist countries are being subjected to a similar process of economic and financial discipline by these agencies as a condition for loans and other economic assistance (Deacon et al., 1997, Chapter 4, *passim*). Through trade negotiations under GATT and now through the WTO, the entire world is being prepared for increasing commodification and free trade.

One of the objectives is to give MNCs and other business interests a free hand in investing and in organizing production with the least interference or restriction from national governments (Brecher and Costello, 1994, pp. 56–63). For example a major initiative launched recently is the Multilateral Agreement on Investments, or MAI, which was being negotiated secretly through the OECD. Opposition by NGOs and differences among member states have led to its being put on hold for the moment. The main objective of the MAI is to give foreign capital the right to 'national treatment', in effect unrestricted access to do business in countries with virtually no accountability to or restriction by national governments (Clarke and Barlow, 1997).

In the case of industrialized countries the pressure for deregulation, commodification and privatization comes from the OECD and IMF largely in the form of expert advice, recommendations and the ongoing evaluation of economic and social policies of nations.[4] However, OECD policies can also take the form of binding decisions on member states. Such was the case, for example, with the code which provides for the free movement of capital across member countries (Ley and Poret, 1997; OECD, 1995a).

It is no secret that the IMF and OECD have been exhorting European welfare states to move further towards the neoliberal approach of the US and UK. Thus Europeans are chastised routinely for maintaining labour market 'rigidities' – a barrier to economic adaptation and change in the context of international competition (OECD, 1994a, pp. 29–31). These so-called 'rigidities', supposedly responsible for 'Eurosclerosis', are a euphemism for programmes of social protection built up in European countries over nearly a century. Thus according to the IMF, the greater flexibility of the labour market in the United States consists in

> less generous unemployment insurance provision in terms of benefit payments, duration of benefits, and qualifications of benefits; wider earnings dispersions; lower levels of unionisation and less centralised wage bargaining; less government intervention in the wage bargaining process; fewer restrictions on hiring and firing of employees; and lower social insurance charges and other non-wage labour costs, such as the amount of paid vacation (IMF, 1994, p. 36).

What is demanded then in the name of 'flexibility' is nothing short of a scaling down, if not dismantling, of measures aimed at protecting workers' living standards and humanizing working conditions. From the standpoint of international competitiveness and economic growth, these appear as impediments to the swift and profitable deployment of labour (CEC, 1993, pp. 136–8). Flexibility, in short, is but another name for the commodification of labour. The influential OECD (1994a) report on labour markets and employment, 'The Jobs Study', echoes these concerns about 'rigidity' which it sees as a major cause of unemployment.

Structural unemployment in OECD countries, the report asserts, was a result of the 'gap between the pressures on economies to adapt to change and their ability to do so' (ibid., p. 7). Policies and systems had made OECD economies 'rigid and stalled [their]… ability and even willingness to adapt' (ibid.). The 'erosion of the ability to adapt to change was probably most pronounced in Continental Europe and Oceania' (ibid., p. 30). While public sector employment grew in Europe, 'impediments to private sector hiring increased, as the incentive to accept work – particularly low-paying or precarious work – diminished, and as societies demanded more publicly-provided services' (ibid.). Albeit tempered by some concern about the growth of low-wage employment, the US is held up virtually as a model of 'flexibility' and 'adaptation'. The report notes that the US has had 'a different response to new technology and globalization. Protective labour market and social policies were [less] extensive; labour markets remained highly flexible; and enterpreneurship was dynamic' (ibid.).

Apart from labour market 'flexibility', the OECD report also emphasizes the importance of controlling inflation and reducing budget deficits. Moreover, deficits are to be reduced by cutting expenditures rather than increasing taxes, given the high tax burden in many OECD countries and 'widespread political resistance to further tax increases' (OECD, 1995b, p. 17). Raising the retirement age, reducing pension benefits and increasing pension contributions are advocated as possible ways of dealing with the consequences of an ageing population. The reduction of unemployment benefits and the restructuring of social assistance are seen as important in removing disincentives to job searches and to the acceptance of low-wage work (ibid., p. 25). Indeed the report discusses social policy quite extensively proffering general advice along these lines to member countries.

New Zealand provides a good example of the role of the OECD and IMF in promoting deregulation and privatization in individual countries. The drastic reforms in New Zealand which began in 1984 and continued into the early 1990s changed its economy from being one of the most closed to one of the most open among OECD countries. These reforms were along the lines favoured by the OECD and IMF (Kelsey, 1995, p. 197).

Indeed for these agencies New Zealand became something of a test case for implementing neoliberal market reforms (Massey, 1995, pp. 71, 157). The OECD evaluated these reforms and the subsequent economic performance of the country in glowing terms and remonstrated with governments for not carrying projected changes far enough. It noted that the sharp reduction in rates of income taxation, especially top rates, had turned New Zealand's tax system into 'one of the least distorting in the OECD' (Orr, 1995, p. 52). On the Employment Contracts Act of 1991 which practically abolished collective bargaining, the OECD's comment was that it had made New Zealand's labour market 'one of the most liberal'. Meanwhile, it noted that decline in union membership had greatly accelerated, making 'wage determination and employment conditions markedly more flexible' (ibid.). New Zealand's international competitiveness and trade performance were seen as having 'improved significantly'. Admitting that these changes involved short-term pain, the report asserts that they are sure to bring long-term gain (ibid., p. 53).

While neoliberal reforms are lauded and their consequences seen as most beneficial, the success of social market economies is glossed over, if not downplayed, and negative features are sought out and emphasized. For example, the contrast in the OECD's assessment of the economic performance and policies of the US, the UK and New Zealand on the one hand and Germany, Sweden and other Continental European economies on the other suggests value judgement rather than objectivity.[5]

The OECD's economic surveys of member countries routinely monitor and review social policy, offering 'sage' advice and occasionally stern warnings. The general thrust of recommended changes is towards making labour markets and economies more 'flexible', reducing government debt and deficit by slashing social spending while maintaining low levels of taxation. Benefits such as unemployment insurance and social assistance are singled out for particular attention since they 'distort' labour markets and prevent 'adaptation' to change.

In sum it would be a mistake to think of globalization as simply a market-driven phenomenon. The supranational steering of the economic and social policy of nations by influential IGOs in a broadly neoliberal direction must be regarded as central to the process of globalization. Indeed it is this politics of transnational social policy that explains in part why globalization is virtually synonymous with monetarism and neoliberalism. As Martin (1994, p. 61) points out there are 'no more transnational markets without politics than there are national ones, but the politics are different. They are inter-state politics'. Put simply, what Martin seems to be saying is that since it is the US – despite some decline in its hegemonic role – rather than say Germany or Japan, that remains the most influential world power, it is the ideological preferences of the US that are inscribed in transnational economic policies. In the absence of a world government, transnational economic and social policies are under the sway of the leading world power. Indeed it is no secret that the US remains the dominant influence in international agencies such as the IMF and WB. Albert (1993) too finds that the neoliberal version of capitalism is in ascendancy over other, e.g. German and Japanese, versions. But for Albert, the reasons are largely cultural and ideological. It is the 'seductive power' of the American model that accounts for its growing popularity (ibid., p. 169).

DECENTRING THE NATION STATE

The welfare state developed as and still remains very much a national enterprise. Historically the objectives of national integration and nation-building have been important in the development of collective social provision. In Europe at the turn of the century, acute national rivalries associated with imperialism provided a strong impetus to ruling elites to offer concessions to the lower classes. Reforms were intended to fashion a sense of national unity and national purpose demanded by economic and military competition. In Britain, for example, the national efficiency movement led to greater state involvement in promoting the education and health of the nation's children. After WW2 the full employment universal welfare state institutionalized the idea of 'one nation' by way of social citizenship. Moreover, tripartism and other similar arrangements were aimed at securing the co-operation of key economic players within the framework of the nation state in order to achieve national objectives.

In countries such as Canada, universal social programmes underpinned the sense of solidarity of a nation made up of diverse regions, two founding peoples and a sparse population spread across a vast land mass (Myles, 1996, p. 130; McBride and Shields, 1997). Indeed the idea of maintaining and consolidating the national community – economically, politically and socially – was the ideological underpinning par excellence of the welfare state.

As we approach the millennium the nation state seems to be in retreat. A resurgent globalization is increasingly blurring the economic boundaries of the nation state. Capital's freedom to move across the globe, the growth of multinational corporations and the transnational production of goods and services are marginalizing the nation as the site for economic organization and activity. As global sceptics have rightly argued, the idea that MNCs no longer have a national identity and interest is an exaggeration and it is more accurate to speak of greater internationalization rather than globalization of economies (Wade, 1996, p. 61; Hirst and Thompson, 1996, p. 16).

But there is little doubt that globalization has strengthened the hands of capital against the nation state. With growing free trade and the freedom to locate abroad, substantial sections of capital may have far less stake in the nation state. Neither domestic markets nor the domestic labour supply have the same significance as they had in the heyday of the welfare state. The weakening, if not decline of tripartism in European countries generally shows that in a globalizing economy, capital does not need labour's co-operation in part because for the former, the national economic framework is no longer the defining reality.

The return of unemployment, the decentralization of collective bargaining and the recommodification of labour markets are undermining the 'one nation' approach to economic and social issues which characterized the era of the welfare state. As often, the US shows in an extreme form a trend that may be growing, at least in Anglo-Saxon countries, if not more widely. In the US, apparently, economic elites no longer feel as connected with the rest of the nation as they once did. Affluent America is tending to withdraw into enclaves protected by private security guards and alarm systems with little concern for the fate of the rest of Americans (Reich, 1992, pp. 268–74; Rifkin, 1995, p. 212).

With globalization dividing societies increasingly into winners and losers, the concept of 'national interest' is becoming difficult to sustain and the concept of a national community is in danger of becoming 'increasingly empty' (Horsman and Marshall, 1995, p. 221). The question is whether, in the absence of a strong sense of a shared identity and interest in nationhood, the welfare state can survive as anything other than an institutional legacy of the past in the process of gradual decay.

The growth of regional economic associations such as the EU, NAFTA and others is yet another development weakening the sovereignty and autonomy of nation states. Whether these associations should be seen as an aspect of globalization, a regional response to it or an autonomous development is a debatable issue and will not be pursued here. What is not in doubt, however, is that these associations are here to stay and they restrict the sovereignty of nations with regard to fiscal, monetary and social policy. For example under the Maastricht Treaty the EU has laid down stringent conditions for membership in the European monetary union. These include keeping budget deficits within 3 per cent of GDP, accumulated national debts within 60% of GDP and inflation within certain specified limits. For many EU countries, reaching deficit targets has already meant a sizeable reduction in social expenditure since increased taxation is an unlikely option.

Major European countries such as France and Germany, in trying to meet the Maastricht criteria on deficits, have seen massive protests and demonstrations against policies of austerity and social retrenchment (see pp. 68–9). True, member states are free to pursue their own social policy and apart from the modest Social Charter, concerned with workers' rights and not legally binding as a whole, the EU has little by way of a common European social policy. On the other hand the economic policies of the EU are indirectly imposing significant constraints on the social policy of member countries.

NAFTA, with the US, Canada and Mexico as members, differs in many respects from the EU. For one thing the United States is the overwhelmingly dominant member and thus the most influential partner. For another, unlike the EU, NAFTA has no aspirations towards an economic and political union of member states. The network of social protection in the US is less well developed than in Canada, while Mexico has a much lower level of wages and social protection. There are no social policy provisions as such in NAFTA and member states are nominally free to follow their own social policies.

But this freedom is somewhat illusory. Economic provisions of NAFTA are meant to establish 'a level playing field' for competition in North America which includes the elimination of 'non-tariff' barriers. And although existing state services have been exempted, NAFTA places definite restrictions on the further development of social protection through the public sector. Measures judged to establish a monopoly in the supply of services or their subsidization are likely to be struck down. Moreover the influence of American neo-conservative ideology is strong and pervasive. Indirectly, therefore, NAFTA's free trade and competition policies restrict the sovereignty and autonomy of member countries to choose their own social and economic policies. Since NAFTA is meant to encourage competition, regulatory and interventionist policies suffer the most. The Chiapas uprising in Mexico is a poignant reminder of the social impact of NAFTA's economic policies. In Canada the influence of NAFTA seems to be towards social dumping and a strong pressure for the downward harmonization of social protection policies.

In sum the sovereignty and autonomy of nation states are being curtailed through globalization and the growth of regional economic associations. Although the latter – as can be seen in the case of the EU – have the potential to develop supranational social policy, this possibility seems to be rather limited. On the other hand the potential of regional associations for economic deregulation and downward pressure on standards of social protection of member states would seem to be greater (Leibfried and Pierson, 1995a; see pp. 128–9 below).

It is something of a paradox that we speak of the decline of the nation state at a time when in fact their numbers are multiplying. Moreover the desire for autonomy and nationhood on the part of linguistic and ethnic communities remains as strong as ever. Nonetheless globalization and regionalization are processes that are restricting the freedom of nations and sub-national units to pursue autonomous monetary, fiscal and social policies. At the same time, however, we also see national governments facilitating and promoting globalization (Czerny, 1997).

These are contradictory tendencies, but the contradiction is more apparent than real. Globalization and regionalization are limiting the range of choices available to nation states but only relatively, and then in respect of particular areas of policy. This still leaves nation states and other jurisdictions with a good deal of policy autonomy in respect of cultural, social and also many economic matters. Moreover, as we argued above, globalization must be seen as a form of transnational neoliberalism. It is the nation state that has to implement the agenda of liberalization and deregulation. Indeed neo-conservative regimes may be expected to go about this with considerable élan. And in this sense it would be correct to see national actors as facilitating and furthering globalization (Czerny, 1997, p. 251). It is also the case that the nation state as a linguistic, cultural and political community remains very much alive and real for the mass of the population which, after all, has no global identity. In this sense, again, nationhood and nationalism are not in decline.

However, and this is important for the welfare state, if the incentive for and the prospect of *nation-building* through collective social provision are weaker in today's world it is mainly because of globalization. Thus Japan in the 1970s and Korea in the 1980s seemed poised to develop more universalistic and encompassing social policies, somewhat along the lines of Western welfare states (Goodman and Peng, 1996, pp. 203–8; Pempel, 1989, pp. 153–4). However, a number of factors, including increasing international competition, economic volatility and neoconservative ascendancy in the West have inhibited this development.[6] In general, then, nationhood and democracy are in conflict with the economic trends and tendencies privileged by globalization. How this conflict is working out in practice and what it means for social policy are matters to be explored in subsequent chapters.

SOCIAL POLICY AND THE 'LOGIC' OF GLOBALIZATION

Of the three interrelated and overlapping developments outlined above, it is globalization that is the focus of our inquiry. If the collapse of the socialist alternative is a cause of globalization, the decline of the nation state is an effect. Globalization, which must be understood as an economic as well as a political and ideological phenomenon, is without a doubt now the essential context of the welfare state.

In the following three chapters (2, 3 and 4), we explore the relationship between globalization and social policy in some detail. The framework of this exploration is the 'logic' of globalization, i.e. given the nature of globalization as an economic process (albeit driven by politics and ideology), what are the likely consequences for the welfare state? The following propositions seek to spell out this logic in relation to social policy and social welfare.

1. Globalization undermines the ability of national governments to pursue the objectives of full employment and economic growth through reflationary policies. 'Keynesianism in one country' ceases to be a viable option.
2. Globalization results in an increasing inequality in wages and working conditions through greater labour market flexibility, a differentiated 'post-Fordist' work-force and decentralized collective bargaining. Global competition and mobility of capital result in 'social dumping' and a downward shift in wages and working conditions.
3. Globalization exerts a downward pressure on systems of social protection and social expenditure by prioritizing the reduction of deficits and debt and the lowering of taxation as key objectives of state policy.
4. Globalization weakens the ideological underpinnings of social protection, especially that of a national minimum, by undermining national solidarity and legitimating inequality of rewards.
5. Globalization weakens the basis of social partnership and tripartism by shifting the balance of power away from labour and the state and towards capital.
6. Globalization constrains the policy options of nations by virtually excluding left-of-centre approaches. In this sense it spells the 'end of ideology' as far as welfare state policies are concerned.
7. The logic of globalization comes into conflict with the 'logic' of the national community and democratic politics. Social policy emerges as a

major issue of contention between global capitalism and the democratic nation state.

Propositions 1 and 2 are the subject matter of Chapter 2, which looks at the employment and labour market implications of a globalizing economy. Propositions 3 and 4 are the focus of Chapter 3, which is primarily concerned with social protection and social expenditure. Propositions 5, 6 and 7 are the subject matter of Chapter 4, which considers the response of national politics to the pressures of globalization. Although these chapters are based largely on developments in Anglo-Saxon countries, the situation in Continental Europe and elsewhere is also referred to, emphasizing the differences between these different types of welfare capitalism. Chapter 5 considers these differences in some detail with special reference to developments in Sweden, Germany and Japan.

Chapter 6 revisits the propositions outlined above in light of the arguments and evidence presented in earlier chapters. It concludes that if there is a logic of globalization it is rather a weak one and on the whole, unregulated/deregulatory globalization represents a neoliberal approach to international political economy. Important cross-national differences in types of capitalism and models of welfare persist and thus far, seem compatible with economic globalization.

However the long-term survival of these different models is by no means assured. The process of globalization is being extended further through the liberalization of trade, investment and the transnational production of goods and services. Moreover, influential IGOs are likely to reinforce the trend towards the globalization of markets and privatization. Although counter-tendencies in the form of emerging contradictions and social conflicts are also at work, thus far they remain somewhat muted (see pp. 107–9). In any case the need for regulating globalization and ensuring that the economic juggernaut of global capitalism does not trample social development under its wheels is obvious. In closing, therefore, Chapter 7 argues for a transnational approach to social standards, i.e. the institutionalization of standards of social protection world-wide by linking social standards firmly to economic development.

NOTES

1. As a concept, globalization invites comparison with such broad-gauge notions as modernization, industrialization, secularization and privatization. In short, it is open-ended, multifaceted and subject to a variety of interpretations. Of the many aspects of globalization, for example economic, political and cultural, it is the economic aspect and the political economy of globalization that we shall be concerned with.

There is a vast and growing literature on globalization. For a general introduction and overview see Waters (1995). On economic aspects Wade (1996) provides an excellent overview. For more detailed examination of the economics and the political economy of globalization see, for example, Ohmae (1990), Boyer and Drache (1996) and Hirst and Thompson (1996). On political aspects see, for example, Held (1995) and Czerny (1997). Rhodes (1996) provides a useful overview of the relation between globalization and the welfare state from a European perspective; see also Kosonen (1998).

2.   For a highly optimistic view of social democracy's continuing viability and effectiveness in conditions of globalization see Garrett (1998). Garrett's argument, however, has a number of limitations. First, he limits his attention to *corporatist* social democracies of Northern Europe and has little to say about the prospects of social democracy more generally. Second, he seeks to demonstrate his thesis of social democratic viability with reference to the period 1966–90 which he sees as one of increasing internationalization of economies. However, as he himself recognizes, the crucial variable has been the removal of capital controls and financial liberalization, a much more recent phenomenon in Nordic countries and Austria. His brief survey of the post-1990 period shows corporatist social democracy to be in a weaker position, with high unemployment and tax regressivity (ibid., Chapter 6). We return to the question of left politics and its current relevance later (see Chapter 6 of this text).

3.   The fact that nation states may initiate the globalization of economies has been taken by global sceptics as evidence of the continuing autonomy and relevance of the nation state as a decision-making body. This is based on the erroneous notion of a zero-sum relationship between the nation state and globalization. Once the ideological and political dimensions are brought in, then globalization can be seen as a *process* driven by a variety of political and economic actors such as national governments, corporations, IGOs and others. As Weiss (1997, p. 20) points out, nation states have acted in the past and are acting today 'as catalysts for the "internationalisation" strategies of corporate actors'. Moreover 'it is not the state as such which is enfeebled by economic integration ... it is the efficacy of specific *policy instruments* which is in question' (ibid., p. 21). In other words it is more a question of the nation state's autonomy being curtailed in some areas and aspects of policy, than the loss of autonomy tout court. On the relationship between globalization and the nation state see Hirst and Thompson (1996), Weiss (1997) and (1998), and Czerny (1997).

4.   See for example *World Economic Outlook*, the bi-annual survey of IMF, and IMF *Staff Papers*. On OECD see the economic surveys of individual member states as well as special reports and studies. On unemployment and labour market flexibility, see OECD (1994a) and IMF (1994, p. 36; IMF, 1997, pp. 4–5). Ministerial and other meetings held under the auspices of these organizations provide an important channel for influencing policy.

5.   See for example OECD (1996a) and (1997e) economic surveys of New Zealand and Germany, respectively.

6.   Since the beginning of the 1980s, Japan has emphasized reliance on non-state sectors – the extended family, the company and the community – for welfare (Goodman and Peng, 1996, pp. 193–4, 208: Watanuki, 1986). However, expenditure apart, there has been some expansion in state welfare lately such as the Chronic Care Insurance programme for the aged (Peng, 1999, p. 12). Peng finds a swing back towards state provision in the 1990s partly due to the declining role of corporate welfare (ibid., pp. 15–16). Globalization may, indeed, be undermining the Japanese 'way' of welfare (see Chapter 5). In Korea the recent (1997–98) financial crisis, followed by IMF loans and conditionalities, may slow down or reverse the growth of social protection. On the other hand, high unemployment and reduced economic growth would underline the need for social protection in the 'tiger' economies. The effects of globalization on East Asian welfare regimes are examined in, for example, Wad (1998) and Hort and Kuhnle (1998).

2. Employment, labour market and income: growing insecurity and inequality

This chapter will examine developments in respect of employment, the labour market and income distribution in Western industrial countries since about the late 1970s. It begins with a brief look at the idea of full employment and its significance for the post-WW2 welfare state. It then traces the subsequent demise of full employment and the rise of unemployment and looks at some of the major remedies being proposed in official circles to deal with the problem. This is followed by an examination of the changing labour market and the resulting implications for wages, income distribution and occupational benefits. The consequences of globalization and changing technology for the above developments are a major underlying theme of this chapter.

THE END OF FULL EMPLOYMENT

Arguably, full employment was a crucial underpinning of the post-WW2 welfare state. It was, of course, one of the basic assumptions of the Beveridge plan for abolishing want. It is not difficult to see why. Since employment was the major source of income for the vast majority of the working-age population and their dependants, some form of full employment (albeit chiefly affecting male breadwinners) was the first source of income guarantee and maintenance. The Keynesian welfare state (KWS), which came into being largely in response to the human and financial costs of mass unemployment, was insistent on this.

There was also a political element involved. Communism, an alternative form of social system and a serious challenger to capitalism, had abolished unemployment and guaranteed the right to work to everyone. Moreover, the interwar years had shown the radical implications of mass unemployment in the form of industrial unrest, political instability, the rise of fascism and a general threat to the social order of capitalism.

These were weighty considerations. More specifically, the experience of unemployment insurance in the interwar years had shown (at any rate in

Britain, the country with the most extensive form of unemployment insurance) that mass unemployment put a huge strain on the public purse (Bruce, 1965, pp. 228–38). For, on the one hand the state lost revenue (taxes and contributions from the unemployed) and on the other had to spend more on benefits – unemployment insurance or social assistance – for the unemployed and their dependants. This 'double whammy' weakened state finances in the long run. For these and other reasons, securing high levels of employment through demand management and fine tuning of the market economy was a key component of the post-WW2 welfare state (ibid., pp. 278–9).

Through a combination of favourable factors and with the help of Keynesian demand-management techniques, the quarter century after WW2 saw conditions of full employment – or something approaching it – throughout the industrialized West. Communist countries, meanwhile, maintained full employment as a part of the Marxist creed of a socialized economy. Thus during the period 1960–73, unemployment in OECD countries averaged 3.25 per cent and annual economic growth a spectacular 4.9 per cent (OECD, 1988, p. 39). Overall full employment, economic growth and expanding social programmes formed a positive-sum relationship from which each benefited.[1] True, there were both national and regional variations in commitment to full employment. The manner in which full employment was maintained also varied.

Sweden, for example, developed an extensive labour market policy as a back-up to full employment which, among other things, ensured that the maintenance of full employment would not be at the cost of low productivity and technological stagnation or a dual economy. From the late 1960s the expansion of the public services provided a major new source of employment, especially for women. Japan used a very different approach based on something like a dual labour market. In large corporations a system of lifetime or permanent employment for core employees co-existed with temporary employment for others. Outside large corporations, employment was less secure with fewer benefits, but within a national policy of full employment. In North America – both Canada and the US – levels of unemployment were a good deal higher than in Europe and Australasia, as the commitment to full employment was weaker.[2]

The events that followed the OPEC price shock are well known. Unemployment began to rise in industrial nations. The so-called trade-off between unemployment and inflation (the Phillips Curve) ceased to work as Western economies faced a situation of continuing inflation in the midst of recession and unemployment. In any case by the early 1980s neoliberal ideas about the efficient functioning of the market economy began to gain ground and governments of the rightist persuasion abandoned the goal of maintaining full employment as they embraced monetarism and high interest rates to fight inflation. However, others did not give up on full employment – and they were not all social democratic governments – choosing to fight inflation through means other than monetarism and unemployment.

Chief among alternative strategies was that of neocorporatism, whether tripartite or bipartite, which relied on dialogue and consensus among social partners for moderating wage rises, containing inflation and maintaining competitiveness (Mishra, 1990). Austria and Sweden offer good examples of the effective use of this strategy in the 1970s and 1980s, while Japan had its own distinctive approach to full employment (Therborn, 1986, pp. 101–11; Schregle, 1993). Thus some countries were able to maintain a high level of employment even in the 1980s, while Japan maintained full employment (unemployment less than 3 per cent) until the mid-1990s (OECD, 1998, p. 246).

GLOBALIZATION AND THE RETURN OF UNEMPLOYMENT

In the late 1970s it looked as though there was a choice between taking the road to monetarism and unemployment or to neocorporatism and full employment (Mishra, 1984, Chapter 4). With the increasing globalization of the economy – notably the relaxation and eventual abolition of government control over capital mobility, flexible exchange rates and the commodification of money and currency – the Keynesian approach of reflating the economy to stimulate growth and job creation became untenable.

An early example of this was seen in France in 1981 when the Mitterand Government tried to use the strategy of reflation to stimulate employment and growth. It had to beat a hasty retreat in 1982 chiefly due to the openness of the economy and international financial pressures (Hall, 1987; Sassoon, 1996, pp. 548–61). In corporatist Sweden as capital controls were relaxed, the trade-off between wage moderation and employment came unstuck. Business found it more advantageous to invest abroad rather than at home and to scuttle the centralized system of wage bargaining (Stephens, 1996, pp. 49–50). Meanwhile public sector jobs as a source of employment began to shrink as pressure began to build to reduce the tax burden and to downsize the state sector.

Although social partnership and a consensus-based approach to industrial relations and economic management remain a part of the political economy of many European countries, the essential point to be made here is that with the collapse of the Bretton Woods system and the subsequent liberalization of the world economy, the preconditions for creating full employment through 'reflation in one country' have disappeared. This still leaves the possibility of international Keynesianism, i.e. major world economies such as the US, Japan and Germany could reflate together in order to promote growth and employment. However the prospects of such co-ordinated action seem remote (see Chorney, 1996, pp. 373–5).

Thus unemployment has become a persistent phenomenon in Western industrial countries as well as in former communist countries. Currently over 35 million people, or around 7 per cent of the labour force in OECD countries are unemployed. Some of the unemployment is cyclical and thus there is some fluctuation in the rate of unemployment. Unemployment declined in the second half of the 1980s following the end of the recession of the early 1980s. But the boom ended in 1990 and unemployment rose once again. However, a good deal of unemployment is now 'structural', i.e. non-cyclical and persistent.

A major difference between the three regions of Europe, North America and Japan is in the level as well as duration of unemployment. Long-term unemployment is higher in Europe as is the rate of unemployment itself (OECD, 1997a, pp. 12–13). To what extent these figures reflect differences in the system of unemployment insurance (for example with more generous and longer-lasting benefits in Europe a larger number of people remain registered as unemployed and for a longer period) and method of counting the unemployed is a matter of contention and debate (see for example, Balls, 1994, p. 47; Thurow, 1996, p. 165; Nickell, 1997).[3] At any rate it appears that in the US there is a large turnover in jobs with huge job losses as well as huge gains. In Europe by contrast the employment situation is far more stable, with far fewer new jobs created and not many old jobs destroyed.

The apparently far superior performance of the US in the creation of new jobs (largely a quantitative rather than qualitative achievement, since the majority are low-paying full-time or part-time jobs with little security and few benefits, a subject to which we shall return) has been attributed to the 'flexibility' of the US labour market. Indeed for quite some time now international agencies, e.g. the OECD and IMF, have been advising European countries to emulate the US and deregulate their labour markets as a means of job creation and 'adaptation' to changing economic and market conditions. Generous unemployment benefits, employment protection measures, high payroll taxes and social security contributions by employers are seen as some of the major forms of 'rigidities' creating disincentives for hiring and dismissal.

One European country that has followed the US example and gone a long way in making its labour market flexible is Britain. Yet the results in terms of employment and job creation have not been impressive. Real rates of unemployment remain much higher than the official rate would have us believe. Most of the new jobs created have been part-time, held chiefly by married women with husbands in full-time work (McLaughlin, 1994, pp. 17–18). On the other hand hundreds of thousands of full-time jobs in manufacturing have disappeared since 1980. As in the US, jobs with low wages and few benefits are proliferating (Elliott, 1997, p. 7; McLaughlin, 1994, p. 14).

The point is that what international agencies are advocating is a simple market model which regards labour power as a commodity. The assumption is that with deregulation more people will be hired, since wages and other non-wage costs of employers will go down. However, Continental Europe with its strong tradition of regulation and étatisme, social democracy and an influential union movement has moved but little towards deregulation. Meanwhile unemployment remains high in most OECD countries and there is no sign that it is likely to come down much in the near future.[4]

Apart from labour market 'flexibility', the other approach to combating unemployment in advanced industrial countries is through education and training. The assumption here is that of a mismatch between the skills and expertise required by a high-technology economy and the existing level of skills of the majority of the working population (for a Canadian perspective see Barlow and Campbell, 1995, pp. 176–80). The solution is seen as consisting in more education, more training and retraining for the jobs of the future.

This is an approach especially in favour in North America. The Clinton administration in the US, for example, regards education and training as the panacea for the problem of unemployment and low wages. Canada takes a similar view (see Rifkin, 1995, p. 36 on the US; Barlow and Campbell, 1995, pp. 170–80 and Osberg et al., 1995, pp. 181–5 on Canada). Yet available evidence does not support this 'trickle-down technology' scenario on jobs in the post-industrial economy. In fact there is only a limited demand for jobs which require a high level of education and training. The majority of jobs being created are service jobs with low skill requirements such as gas-pump attendants, checkout cashiers, fast-food workers, security guards, sales clerks and janitors (Barnet and Kavanagh, 1994, pp. 292–3; Rifkin, 1995, pp. 165–8). Professional and technical jobs are also growing but their numbers will remain small.

The OECD report of 1994, 'Jobs Study' (discussed on p. 9), seems to have endorsed the view that a mismatch of skills was one of the causes of unemployment. The evidence from North America, however, shows quite clearly that there is in fact a glut of well-educated young people who are either unemployed or have to take jobs well beneath the level of their competence (Osberg et al., 1995, pp. 184–5; Mishel and Bernstein, 1994, pp. 16–18). Conversely, surveys show that with minor exceptions, employers are able to find plenty of qualified people to fill vacancies (Osberg et al., 1995, pp. 181–2, 184). Not surprisingly, the 'mismatch of skills' and 'training as a panacea' views of unemployment are heard rather less these days. True, the chances of someone with tertiary education being unemployed are a good deal lower than for someone with elementary education. Individuals therefore seek to upgrade their qualification to be more marketable. But to transfer this individual solution to the national level is to commit an ecological fallacy.

Thus as far as unemployment goes, we are back at 'flexibility' and 'adaptation' as the solution. Put simply, the American 'solution' of 'good jobs (few)/ bad jobs (many)' seems to be the alternative to the Continental European situation of 'good jobs (many)/no jobs (but good unemployment benefits)'. Yet the example of Britain casts doubt on the feasibility of the American solution in smaller economies in conditions of openness and globalization. Little attention has been paid so far to this aspect of lesson-learning from the US.

More ominously, the phenomenon of 'jobless growth' is not only here but is likely to intensify in the coming years. At one time it was believed that just as in the course of industrialization factory work replaced farming and agricultural work, so in the post-industrial economy service jobs would replace manufacturing jobs as the latter disappeared with automation. While to some extent this happened during the post-WW2 decades, current evidence as well as projections of future employment suggest that as the technological revolution – automation through the use of computers and microelectronics – gathers pace, jobs are also likely to disappear in the services sector.

A recent authoritative study of the future of work (Rifkin, 1995) symptomatically entitled 'The End Of Work' argues convincingly along these lines. Productivity is now rising so fast that services are likely to follow in the footsteps of agriculture and industry in being able to sustain a large output with a small work-force. The 'workless' economy is already on the horizon. One need not go all the way with this somewhat technocratic argument which in any case takes a long-term view of the labour market. Yet the direction it points to is quite clear. Freer trade, capital mobility and world-wide competition seem to have speeded up technological change enormously. And there are enough data on hand to show that indeed we are now involved in jobless growth or at best, growth with low-paid and precarious employment. Even as the turnover and profits of corporations increase, they are engaged in downsizing the labour force aggressively.

While the economy grows, profits rise and the stock market surges ahead, unemployment, instead of falling, keeps rising. Or at best, as in the US, secure and well-paid jobs are eliminated and replaced by a plethora of part-time and insecure jobs. The assumptions underlying the Keynes–Beveridge approach to unemployment have lost a good deal of their validity in what is not only a post-industrial but also a post-Fordist economy.[5] The positive-sum relationship between economic growth, jobs and wages has ceased to exist. It is clear that the globalization of the economy together with automation and the electronics revolution has put paid to the idea of full employment as envisaged by the architects of the post-WW2 welfare state. Surely it is wishful thinking to believe that OECD countries could provide jobs for the unemployed in the coming years through private sector job creation. Clearly thus far neither national politicians nor intergovernmental organizations such as the OECD and IMF have acknowledged the true nature and seriousness of the problem. Naturally politics, especially electoral politics, is about purveying optimism. Hence politicians cannot help being involved in the pretence that economic growth and private sector job creation will take care of the problem if not tomorrow then the day after.

The plain fact seems to be – yet it is inadmissible – that either countries will have to live with persistent high unemployment or find other, innovative, solutions such as a basic income, work sharing, a shorter work week and third sector (non-profit) employment. Paradoxically, globalization and a rampaging market economy are generating the need for collective social action if civilized conditions of life are to be maintained. For it is quite clear that market measures have no solution for the problem of chronic unemployment in advanced industrial economies.[6]

It is also clear that in a global economy, individual nation states acting on their own will find it extremely difficult to embark on innovative solutions, solutions that could jeopardize their own competitiveness and put them out of line with their competitors. In short, the problem has moved beyond Keynesian and Swedish models and the only 'model' on offer at the moment is the neoliberal model of 'flexibility' and the dehumanization of the labour market. Only transnational action and policies can come to grips with the problem.[7]

THE CHANGING LABOUR MARKET

The golden age of welfare capitalism not only saw full employment of the working-age population (primarily males but also increasingly females), but the jobs were mainly full-time jobs – often in manufacturing and allied industries.[8] Lack of skill was not a barrier to employment as the new mass production industry required a large complement of semi-skilled and un-skilled workers. Alongside full employment, union membership grew in most countries and collective bargaining became more firmly established. Buoyant demand for labour and rising productivity made for good wages, improved working conditions and in countries, e.g. the US, which did not have a developed set of social programmes, also occupational benefits for the work-force. The benefits of economic growth and rising productivity thus accrued to working people (see, for example, Wilensky and Lebeaux, 1965, pp. 100–103; Rifkin, 1995, p. 169).

Thus full employment combined with Fordist methods of production and industrial relations made for reasonably secure, full-time jobs with good wages and benefits. True, Fordism was also patriarchal and helped to reproduce the male wage-earner/female home-maker pattern of family wages. But at least it promoted greater equality *between households* and a great deal of income security and stability more generally. What this meant for the system of social welfare was that the economy itself acted as a preventive measure against poverty and want.

This somewhat felicitous state of affairs began to change from about the late 1960s. A variety of factors were involved. First, increasing competition from Japan and the newly industrializing countries which enjoyed significant cost advantages in the mass production of standardized consumer goods meant a decline in employment in the older manufacturing sector. Second, with increasing capital mobility, freedom to locate production overseas and the use of outsourcing, some of the routine production moved out into the Third World. Third, changing technologies and methods of production combined with greater competition took their toll on old smokestack industries. Fourth, the decline in manufacturing employment was exacerbated in some countries, e.g. the US and UK, through deliberate government policies. These included high interest rates, monetarism and the exposure of domestic industries to international competition. The result has been described as 'de-industrialization'. Both countries suffered heavy job losses in manufacturing – the bastion of male full employment in the 1950s and 1960s. In the US, the proportion of the labour force in manufacturing fell from around one-third in 1950 to one-sixth in the 1990s (Barnet and Kavanagh, 1994, pp. 275–6; Rifkin, 1995, p. 8). In the UK manufacturing employment declined by more than a quarter between 1979 and 1990 (Nolan, 1994, p. 64; OECD, 1994b, p. 5). Finally, there was rapid growth in service industries and occupations.

The main point here is that the jobs lost in manufacturing were in the main unionized jobs – well paid and often with good occupational benefits. The bulk of the jobs created in the services are lower paid, often non-unionized and with poor or non-existent workplace benefits. Studies of 'deindustrialization' in the US show, for example, that only a small fraction of displaced workers are able to get jobs which pay comparable wages. It appears that the majority of these workers have suffered a considerable decline in wages since average wages in service occupations tend to be a good deal lower than those in manufacturing (Rifkin, 1995, pp. 166–7; Mishel et al., 1997, p. 185).

More recently, i.e. in the 1980s and 1990s, as international competitiveness has accelerated, companies have changed to 'lean' production. This has meant the substantial growth of 'non-standard' forms of employment including part-time work (Belous, 1989; Mishel and Bernstein, 1994, Chapters 3 and 4; Mishel et al., 1997, Chapter 4). Latest developments point to a 'just in time' or a disposable labour force to match the 'just in time' inventory, which saves the cost of carrying an inventory of goods.

Global competition has made 'flexibility' the watchword of business and industry. Non-standard forms of work arrangements constitute one aspect of labour market 'flexibility'. Thus part-time, temporary and contractual work, home working, sub-contracting and the like have been growing rapidly especially in the US, UK and other Anglo-Saxon countries (on the US see below; on the UK see McLaughlin, 1994, p. 14; on Australia see OECD, 1997b, p. 72). Another form of flexibility concerns wages and other non-wage costs, e.g. workplace benefits. Non-union employment, decentralized collective bargaining and the deregulation of labour relations and working conditions are seen as enhancing the freedom of employers to use labour as a commodity. This is seen as crucial for being cost-effective and competitive in the global market place.

Evidently the US seems to have developed 'flexibility' of this sort to an advanced level, perhaps surpassed only by New Zealand (OECD, 1996a, p. 54). The 'contingent' labour force has shown a rapid growth. During the period 1982–90, for example, the temporary help industry in the US grew ten times as fast as overall employment (Appelbaum, 1992, p. 1). Nearly half of the jobs created in the early 1990s were non-standard part-time jobs compared with about a quarter of new jobs in the 1980s. In 1992, for example, two-thirds of new private sector jobs were temporary. It is estimated that in the early 1990s about 25–30 per cent of the work-force in the US consisted of non-standard workers, a trend that is growing (Rifkin, 1995, p. 191; Kahne, 1994, p. 419).

The loss of manufacturing jobs, the rapid growth of a contingent workforce and the decline of unionization appear to be the main factors responsible for a persistent wage decline and growing wage inequality in the US. As Mishel and Bernstein (1994, pp. 14–15) write, 'The continuing deterioration in the quality of jobs has been the central force challenging the economic well-being of most Americans since 1979. In terms of both wages and benefits, the real hourly pay of most workers was severely eroded from 1979 to 1993'. Indeed this erosion continued into the mid-1990s (Mishel et al., 1997, pp. 3–6, 149).

Apart from low wages, other aspects of the deteriorating quality of jobs are the absence of security of employment and occupational benefits (ibid., pp. 8–10). Thus many 'part-time and temporary jobs fail to provide guaranteed employment, fringe benefits, a living wage, any accommodation of family responsibilities or opportunities for union representation' (du Rivage, 1992, p. 89). Du Rivage suggests that with the expansion of contingent work, 'employer–employee relations have entered a new era in which the responsibilities for health care insurance, an adequate wage, and indeed even job creation, have been shifted to individual workers and their families' (ibid., p. 94). Thus three-quarters of full-year and 88 per cent of part-year but part-time workers were not covered for health insurance at their jobs compared with only 20 per cent of full-year, full-time workers.

Indeed employers are responding to escalating health insurance costs (a) by hiring contingent workers who do not receive health benefits and (b) by shifting costs to workers and their families through such measures as higher deductibles and premiums and reduced benefit coverage (ibid.). Not surprisingly, the percentage of workers covered by health and pension plans shows a decline (OECD, 1997c, p. 96; Mishel et al., 1997, pp. 156–61).

SOCIAL DUMPING

In the United States an important strategy of business in forcing workers to accept low wages and working conditions has been the threat of outsourcing or relocating plants outside the country (Barnet and Kavanagh, 1994, pp. 312–13, 317). American labour's opposition to NAFTA was largely based on the fear of social dumping, i.e. the ratcheting downwards of wages and working conditions, when a country like Mexico, with its low wages and working conditions and absence of union rights becomes part of a common market in the supply of labour as well as goods and services (Grinspun and Cameron, 1993). Canadian workers were afraid on account of both the US and Mexico since working conditions and union rights are superior in Canada and wage levels higher compared with at least the southern states of the US (Stanford et al., 1993).

Overall it remains true that fear of social dumping has proven exaggerated. Neither North America nor the European Union, which also boasts large differences in wages and working conditions, shows any evidence of a large-scale move by industry to low-wage areas (Adnett, 1995). Investment and location decisions have to take a variety of factors into account beside labour costs. Chief among these are access and proximity to markets, availability of a skilled and disciplined labour force, good infrastructure of transport and communications as well as non-economic factors such as political stability and cultural affinity.

It must also be remembered that what really matters is not the absolute but the relative or unit cost of labour, i.e. wages in relation to productivity. Low-wage economies also tend to be low in productivity. Thus the pattern of foreign direct investment over the last two decades shows that roughly three-quarters of investment has flown from one industrialized country to another rather than to low-wage Third World locations (Dicken, 1992, p. 54; Hirst and Thompson, 1996, pp. 67–8). The situation is far more complex than that suggested by a simple thesis of social dumping (Goodhart, 1993). Nonetheless, in an open and competitive economy the prospects of social dumping are real. Both North America and Western Europe offer some evidence to support the social dumping hypothesis (see for example Stanford et al., 1993 on North America; Adnett, 1995, and Leibfried and Pierson, 1994 on the European Union). Incidentally, one of the main objectives of the Social Charter of the EU was to guard against such a possibility.

To sum up: the 'Fordist' labour market typical of the post-WW2 welfare state is giving way to a more 'flexible' and fragmented labour market where average wages, benefits and job security are lower than was typical of the Fordist era. Much of our evidence has been drawn from the US but similar trends can be seen at least in most of the English-speaking countries. If the evidence from the US is an indicator of the logic of globalization at work, it is clear that employers can no longer be relied upon to provide workers with good wages and benefits such as health insurance and pensions. Increasingly workers and their families are being left to fend for themselves, which they are less able to do in a situation of job insecurity and declining wages.

True, governments have been trying to deal with the situation by mandating a measure of employer obligation and responsibility. The Clinton administration, for example, has passed a law which entitles employees to 12 weeks of unpaid leave per year for medical or family reasons (Peele, 1996, p. 329). More recently, a similar measure enables workers who lose their jobs to continue their health insurance on the same conditions but at their own cost (OECD, 1996b, p. 67). In Australia the Labour Government mandated superannuation coverage by employers, a scheme that was subsequently expanded and consolidated (Castles, 1996, p. 109). These ad hoc measures merely point to the fact that short of allowing the full commodification of labour, there is no alternative to government regulation of the labour market and labour relations.

Arguably, mandating employers to provide benefits may be preferable to state provision of services given the climate of budgetary constraint and smaller government. Yet these regulatory measures re-enact rigidities which may also impede corporations from being competitive and cost-efficient. It is somewhat ironic that the state should be expecting the private sector, i.e. employers, to pick up the tab at the very moment when corporations are anxious to reduce their non-wage costs, notably employee benefits.

Clearly, globalization seems to demand not only the downsizing of state welfare but of corporate welfare as well. How can we expect corporations to shoulder the responsibility for employee benefits in a world of 'no holds barred' competition? Moreover, if governments were to subsidize these operations, would that not be a violation of the principle of free trade and amount to a form of protectionism?

GROWING ECONOMIC INEQUALITY AND SOCIAL POLARIZATION

The three decades after WW2 – the golden age of the welfare state – witnessed a significant improvement in living standards. Full employment, good wages and the growth of social protection helped to secure a measure of redistribution of income and life chances – thus providing security as well as a measure of equity. And although in many countries taxation was more progressive in name than in reality, there was at least an ideological acceptance of the principle of progressivity in taxation which prevented taxes from moving too far in a regressive direction. There was also a measure of economic and social levelling. Universal social services, notably education and health care as well as income security, which catered to both the middle and working classes, helped to create a sense of equality of status through social citizenship.

The post-WW2 welfare state was a remarkable achievement by historic standards. True, some countries, especially Scandinavian social democracies, travelled farther along this route than others. But the general direction was broadly similar, i.e. towards full employment, social security and a national minimum standard of life. It should be emphasized, however, that this reduction of inequality across occupational and class lines left some other forms of social inequality – notably those of gender and race – unaddressed. However, social movements for greater equality and the recognition of diverse social identities which began in the late 1960s suggested that the reduction of inequality across class lines might be extended along the lines of race and gender, thus rounding off the equalization process.

The experience of the last two decades shows that these expectations have not been realized. True, the politics of identity and diversity have come to the fore in public debates, and social inequalities of gender, race and sexual orientation have been addressed to some extent. On the other hand, economic equality across occupational and class lines has regressed. In part this reversal has been the result of the neoconservative counter-revolution which has legitimized the interests of business and economic elites in the name of free market and supply side theories of economic growth and taxation.

With the triumph of neoconservative ideology in the UK and the US in the 1980s, income differentials and inequality became an integral component of the new philosophy of the market and individualism. The most visible celebration of this philosophy was through changes in taxation, especially in English-speaking countries led by the UK and the US. In the name of providing enterprise and the market with the incentives for wealth creation, there has been a massive upward redistribution of incomes, notably in the UK, the US and New Zealand. The neoconservative assault on the egalitarianism of welfare capitalism received a further boost and legitimation from the increasing globalization of economies. It has been reinforced by the collapse of communism and the discrediting of state socialism as a social system.

The extent of social regression as evidenced by the US is truly staggering. Robert Reich (1992, pp. 245–6) explains:

> There have been times in our nation's history when the idea of a progressive income tax was not considered especially radical. In 1917, on the eve of World War I, Woodrow Wilson proposed and Congress enacted a steeply progressive tax code with a top rate on individual incomes of 83 percent. ... It came down later but by 1935 had gone back up to ... 79 percent, now coupled with a tax on inherited wealth. There were loopholes but the effective rate was ... still in the range of 50 percent. [But today, Reich informs us,] the ideal of tax progressivity seems fairly quaint in the United States ... By 1990, America's income-tax rate on its wealthiest citizens was the lowest of any industrialised nation.

Overall the statistics of inequality are well known and will only be referred to briefly here. Not only after-tax incomes but also pre-tax incomes have become highly unequal, especially in Anglo-Saxon nations. The distribution of wealth, which tends to be far more unequal than income distribution, has become more so. In the US for example, income inequality has been increasing since the 1970s. In 1990 the poorest 20 per cent of Americans received 3.7 per cent of the national income, the lowest share since 1954. The richest 20 per cent on the other hand received more than 50 per cent of the national income in 1990, an all-time high. In 1960 chief executives of US corporations were making about 40 times the average wage of the American worker. By 1988 they were making 93 times the average wage. After-tax income inequality rose even more sharply. In 1960 American chief executive officers after-tax pay was only about 12 times that of the average worker. By 1988 it had risen to a whopping 70 times (ibid., pp. 204–5).

Between 1978 and 1990, tax regressivity in the US increased sharply. Payroll and social security taxes went up by 30 per cent while income taxes, especially for high-income earners and the rich, came down. The overall tax rate in the US had not increased since the mid-1960s, but the average American was much more heavily taxed (ibid., p. 260). Had the tax code been even as progressive as in 1977 (already less progressive), the top fifth of Americans would have paid $93 billion more in taxes than they paid in 1989 (ibid.).

Although tax regressivity decreased somewhat in the early 1990s, after-tax income inequality and the concentration of wealth remains far greater than in the early 1980s (Mishel et al., 1997, pp. 106, 283). The share of wealth of the top 1 per cent of American households increased from 33.8 per cent in 1983 to 37.2 per cent in 1992. Over the same period the bottom 80 per cent of households saw their share decline from 18.7 per cent to 16.3 per cent (Mishel et al., 1997, p. 283).

During the period 1979–92 the proportion of Americans working full-time but earning less than a poverty-level income for a family of four (about $13 000 a year) rose by 50 per cent (Rifkin, 1995, p. 169). While stock prices in the 1980s rose nearly 400 per cent, the average weekly wage dropped from $387 in 1979 to $335 in 1989 (ibid., p. 168).

The proportion of Americans with middle incomes fell from 71 per cent of the population in 1969 to less than 63 per cent in the early 1990s. The decline would have been sharper had not two-earner families increased significantly. Even so, median family incomes declined by 2 per cent during 1989–90 (ibid., p. 172) and by 3.4 per cent between 1989 and 1995 (Mishel et al., 1997, p. 41). With real wages dropping, fewer American families are able to buy homes and home ownership in the 1980s declined for prime age-groups (Rifkin, 1995, p. 179).

Clearly the middle class, an emblem of American prosperity and trickle-down economics, is shrinking and the American dream may remain just that for the large majority of new generations of Americans. Rifkin (ibid., p. 173) believes that the 'growing gap in wages and benefits between top management and the rest of the American workforce is creating a deeply polarised America ... with ominous consequences for the future political stability of the nation'.

Statistics from other Anglo-Saxon countries, notably Britain and New Zealand, show a broadly similar trend: a rapid growth in inequality in both before-tax and after-tax incomes and growing social polarization. In the UK, for example, the income gap between the richest and the poorest had narrowed for nearly four decades after WW2. That has now been reversed. 'Today the gap between the earnings of the highest paid and lowest paid workers is greater than at any time since records were first kept in 1886' (CSJ, 1994, p. 28). The deregulation of the labour market along with persistent unemployment, regressive taxation and other inegalitarian measures (e.g. the curb on unions, collective bargaining, etc.) has resulted in increasing inequality, increasing poverty and social degradation, e.g. begging, homelessness and diseases typical of poor countries.

Between 1979 and 1991–92 poverty in Britain nearly tripled, rising from 9 per cent to 25 per cent of the population. Over the period 1979–91/2 the poorest 10 per cent saw their income fall by nearly 20 per cent, whereas the top 10 per cent saw a rise of 60 per cent – the highest gain among the income deciles (ibid., p. 31). Taking all taxes, direct and indirect, into account, the bottom 10 per cent of the population was paying 43 per cent of income in taxes compared with 32 per cent paid by the top 10 per cent (ibid.).

As in the US, job insecurity increased greatly in the UK affecting all classes and not just manual workers. One in three middle-class workers now fears being made redundant next year (ibid., p. 36). Again as in the US, non-standard, including part-time, jobs show a rapid growth in the UK (McLaughlin, 1994, p. 4; OECD, 1994b, p. 9). These jobs are far less likely to pay the kind of benefits available to full-time workers (Hutton, 1995b; Elliott, 1997). In New Zealand the story is the same in rough outlines (Castles, 1996, p. 100; Kelsey, 1995, p. 287; OECD, 1996a, pp. 50, 70).

True, the situation as regards the labour market and income distribution is very different in Continental Europe and also in Japan. Put simply, there is far greater continuity from the past compared with Anglo-Saxon countries (see Chapter 5 of this text). Nonetheless the social systems of these countries are on the defensive. They seem to represent a legacy of the past. Japan's economy, which still remains protected and closed in many respects, is under pressure to open up. The consequences for the Japanese labour market and employment could be far-reaching. European countries are under pressure to deregulate and 'flexibilize' their labour markets and to emulate the US.

In many ways the neoliberal brand of global capitalism is seeking to become hegemonic, at least as far as Western industrial nations are concerned. Thus far, however, Continental Europe has not moved far along the path of deregulation, tax regressivity, inequality and poverty. Does it then mean that such policies have more to do with *national* policies of neoliberalism rather than globalization? And further, that welfare states have little to fear from globalization? We shall return to these important issues later.

SUMMARY AND CONCLUSIONS

This chapter has sought to demonstrate that the neoliberal assault on the KWS followed by the rise of a globalized market economy has weakened the first line of defence against economic insecurity and poverty. Instead of full employment we now have a situation of chronic unemployment, coupled with increasing insecurity of employment. Intensified global competition is revolutionizing technology which in turn is threatening the 'end of work'.

The labour market is also changing in significant ways. In place of full-time jobs with good wages, reasonable job security and occupational benefits, we now see the growth of a contingent work-force – with part-time, temporary and contractual jobs that are often low paid, lack security and provide few benefits.

As a result of increased global competitiveness and the demand for 'flexibility', employer–employee relations are undergoing a major change. Corporate responsibility for the welfare of workers in respect of benefits such as pensions, health care, paid leave and the like is beginning to erode. Anxious to reduce their non-wage labour costs, corporations are in the process of shrinking employee benefits or doing away with them by hiring contingent labour. At the same time the economy is creating increased polarization of incomes and wealth. In the US, for example, the real wages of the work-force have either remained stagnant or declined over the last two decades. The situation in Canada is not dissimilar. Increasingly families are feeling the pinch, although growth in two-earner households is helping to maintain the semblance of a middle-class standard of living.

A significant new development, at least in North America, is that *economic growth is no longer translating into more jobs or higher wages for the majority of the work-force. Clearly, 'trickle-down' is dead.* These developments – chronic unemployment, declining wages and working conditions, job insecurity and diminishing occupational benefits – call into question a number of optimistic assumptions connected with the globalizing market economy. One of these is that a free market economy will – given sufficient time – take care of need and dependency through growth, job creation and higher wages. Another assumption is that as the state withdraws from social provision, the ensuing gap can be filled by non-state sectors, notably employers, the market and voluntary organizations.

As we have seen economic growth of itself need not create more jobs or raise general wages. And in a world of no-holds-barred competition, corporations are subject to the same logic as governments – the need to be lean and mean. And if they are also going to be increasingly footloose, with no sense of identification with any particular community, then we can hardly expect them to be in a position to assume responsibility for employee welfare. Moreover, the fragmentation of the labour force, increasing insecurity of employment and the growth of the contingent work-force are developments that not only put more and more people beyond the pale of corporate benefits but also make it increasingly difficult for individuals and families to fend for themselves.

The point is that these assumptions, let us call them those of (a) trickle-down and (b) welfare pluralism, are really a carry-over from the Keynesian era. But the operations of a global market economy are completely different from those of a predominantly *national* economy. This must be recognized. Neither jobs, nor higher wages, nor social benefits can necessarily be provided by a growing economy.

We therefore reach a paradoxical conclusion. Increasing globalization and competitiveness create economic conditions which require the state or the public sector to play a *more,* not less, important role in social protection. In diminishing the capacity of non-state sectors, especially employers, to provide welfare and at the same time destabilizing and shrinking the income base of a substantial section of the population, a globalized economy leaves the state, whether national or supranational, as the only stable and legitimate organization able to assume responsibility for adequate social protection.

The more the productive sector of the economy is de-socialized, i.e. commodified, the greater is the need for compensatory social policy to provide a measure of equity and a semblance of secure and civilized public life. This might involve the provision of a basic income to compensate for persistent joblessness, income supplementation (in whatever form) for the working poor and adequate pensions and health insurance in the absence of work-related benefits. Moreover, with capital mobility, insecurity of employment, 'lean production', and labour market 'flexibility', the education, training and retraining of the work-force is also far more likely to be the responsibility of the government rather than corporations and employers. Since labour, unlike capital, is not mobile cross-nationally, the upgrading of skills and education must remain a national project – an important responsibility of the national government.

But if a larger role for the state – at least as a co-ordinator and facilitator – appears to be one of the imperatives of globalization, a contradictory imperative seems to be that the social state be downsized and social expenditure reduced. In the next chapter we examine the implications of globalization for state welfare.

NOTES

1. Social expenditure in OECD countries rose from 13.1 per cent of GDP in 1960 to 25.6 per cent in 1981, its annual rate of growth far exceeding that of the GDP (OECD, 1985, p. 21, Table 1).
2. Unemployment in North America (Canada and the US) averaged above 5 per cent for 1960–73 compared with 2.5 per cent for EEC countries and less than 2 per cent for Australia and New Zealand (calculated from OECD, 1988, p. 39, Table 2.15).
3. That the official count of the unemployed in the US seriously underestimates the lack of employment in that country is a widely recognized but little-publicized phenomenon. For example, in 1993 the US Bureau of Labor Statistics put the actual number of unemployed at 16.6 million when the official count was 8.8 million. According to Robert Reich, the Labor Secretary, the official figure was 'grossly inaccurate' (Toinet, 1996, p. 58). In spite of widespread scepticism among scholars, agencies such as the OECD and IMF continue to base their policy recommendations on the official figures.
4. Unemployment in the OECD area was 7.2 per cent in 1997 and was expected to remain at or above 7 per cent for two years (OECD, 1998, p. 8). It varies widely across countries and in 1997 ranged from 2.6 per cent in Korea and 3.4 per cent in Japan at one end to 20.8 per cent at the other in Spain. For the EU countries the rate was 11.2 per cent (ibid., p. 245). The financial turmoil in East Asia and Russia in 1997–8 may push unemployment higher in the OECD area.
5. The Keynes–Beveridge or post-WW2 model of full employment assumed male bread-winners in full-time work, typically in blue-collar industrial work, earning a family wage. Economic growth was supposed to translate into more jobs and higher wages. The post-industrial economy involves a major shift from manufacturing to service employment, which in turn implies other changes, namely in the nature of jobs and their gender composition. Post-Fordism, which overlaps with post-industrialism and globalization, implies a 'flexible' system of production of goods and services based on information technology,

product innovation and decentralized organization of work. The combination of post-Fordism and globalization leads to jobless growth, non-standard forms of employment and greater wage dispersion.

6. By and large, the OECD seems to be sticking to its nostrums on employment put forward in the *Jobs Study* of 1994 (see pp. 9–10), namely greater 'flexibility' of the labour market, more education and training, more stringent benefits policy, active measures to get the unemployed back to work ('workfare'). The US, with its flexible labour market and a plethora of low-wage, low-skill jobs, still remains the exemplar of job creation in a globalized economy (OECD, 1997c) despite the fact that 1 in 4 full-time workers in the US makes less than two-thirds of median earnings (compared for example with less than 1 in 10 in Sweden) (OECD, 1997f, p. 39).

7. The EU, in the context of Maastricht and the monetary union, has made some moves recently towards tackling unemployment which go beyond neoliberal market-based approaches. Member countries are to prepare national action plans on reducing unemployment and the EU is to monitor progress systematically (*Globe and Mail*, 1997, p. A17). Reduction of the work week and encouragement of more voluntary part-time work with the same rights and benefits as full-time work are among the other measures being tried in a number of European countries, e.g. France and the Netherlands. How far these ad hoc measures by individual nations can succeed in reducing unemployment and, more important, in keeping it down remains to be seen. The co-operation of business is also an uncertain element in the equation.

8. For example in the UK, three-quarters of working-age males were in full-time jobs in the early 1970s compared with one-half in the early 1990s (CSJ, 1994, pp. 34, 154).

3. Social policy in retreat or the hollowing out of the welfare state

This chapter is concerned with the consequences of globalization for systems of social protection and social expenditure. The focus is once again on English-speaking countries where both the economics and the ideology of globalization are much in evidence. However, the relationship explored here is 'generic' in nature and the assumption is that other countries are also under pressure to move broadly in the direction taken by Anglo-Saxon countries. How far this assumption is valid and how globalization is playing out in these other countries will be examined in some detail in Chapter 5.

The last chapter tried to show that with the globalization of economies, the first line of defence against poverty and dependency erected by the KWS, i.e. steady economic growth, full employment, good wages and working conditions, has weakened a good deal and is likely to weaken further. The economy is being 'de-socialized' and the labour market recommodified. Chronic unemployment, job insecurity, growth of 'non-standard' jobs – with little security, often low wages and minimal fringe benefits – and growing wage inequality are becoming commonplace.

Now these economic changes need not have an adverse impact on the well-being of people providing an effective system of social protection remains in place. In other words, comprehensive income maintenance and supplementation programmes together with adequate health and welfare services could compensate for the increasing need for social protection resulting from the recommodification of the economy, especially from changes in the labour market and the declining role of employment-related benefits.

Needless to say in most Western industrial countries the basic institutional provisions of the KWS, e.g. unemployment insurance, pensions and medical care remain in place. They are acting to cushion the adverse impact of a globalizing market economy on living standards. But how secure is this system of social protection? Is globalization working against institutionalized social rights and undermining this second line of defence erected by the KWS against deprivation and dependency? And if so, how precisely is this happening? What are the processes involved? The rest of the chapter is an attempt to answer these questions.

DOWNSIZING THE SOCIAL STATE

As far as national debts and budget deficits are concerned, the basic facts are well known and not seriously in dispute. It is also generally recognized that neoliberal policies of monetarism, i.e. fighting inflation with high interest rates, deflation and unemployment have been among the major contributors to the rise in deficits. Moreover, with increasing cross-national mobility of money and capital in the 1980s, interest rates tended to rise everywhere to keep money from flowing out to high-interest countries. This too added to the cost of government borrowing.

With low economic growth, recessions and persistent unemployment, government revenues plummeted while expenditure went up. Furthermore tax breaks to the rich and tax expenditures of various kinds led to loss of revenue. These, rather than excessive government spending, are the main reasons for the rise in budget deficits in Western industrial nations[1] (see for example Osberg and Fortin, 1996 on Canada and Schaeffer, 1997, Chapter 6 on the US).

Deficits, of course, have a cyclical aspect. But although in good years deficits have declined or even disappeared, the resulting accumulated national debt has tended to rise. No doubt, high levels of national debt on which interest has to be paid to lenders (whether domestic or foreign) result in a drag on government finances in so far as a good part of revenue is lost in simply servicing the debt. The need to control deficits and debt therefore remains important. This much is common ground and there is little disagreement about these fundamentals. The crucial question, however, centres around (a) the seriousness of a particular level of debt and deficit for a country, i.e. at what rate should the debt be discharged and (b) the means to be employed in reducing the debt and deficit. This is where globalization comes in.

Just as earlier neoliberalism had privileged the fight against inflation over other goals, so it appears that the globalization of finance and capital has in addition privileged the reduction of debt and deficits over other goals, e.g. sustaining employment, promoting economic growth and maintaining the social safety net. The rationale for deficit reduction is that government borrowing results in the 'crowding out' of private borrowing and investment and that a large national debt means high interest rates. These conditions are detrimental to the economy, i.e. for economic growth and job creation through the private sector. The business and financial community therefore sets great store by deficit reduction.

More particularly, it wants governments to reduce deficits by slashing expenditure rather than raising taxes. Indeed as we shall see later, tax reduction is also one of the policies privileged by globalization. Reducing the deficit then means little more than reducing public (read social) expenditure.

Moreover, for the business community and neoliberals more generally, reducing the deficit becomes almost an obsession with scant regard for its economic and social costs in the form of unemployment, bankruptcies and loss of production.

This is where national capital with its ideology of neoconservatism finds a strong ally in the global market place for pressuring governments into deficit reduction. Moreover the long-term goal of neoliberals is that of achieving a balanced budget and beyond that, one of discharging the accumulated national debt (on Canada, for example, see Barlow and Campbell, 1995, pp. 47–9, 54–5). These long-term objectives of balancing the budget, reducing the national debt and reducing taxation mean that policy is weighted heavily against public spending.

In a sense there is nothing new about these neoliberal objectives. They have been around since the late 1970s. What is new is that financial deregulation and the mobility of money and capital have transformed neoliberalism from a political ideology within a nation state to a policy imperative of global capitalism. True, there is some difference between governments of the Left and Right in this respect. The former tend to follow this policy stance reluctantly – often protesting and complaining about the influence of financial markets against which they feel helpless. The latter tend to be eager followers, if not initiators, who see the attitudes of the global economic and financial community as simply their own economic philosophy writ large. Whatever the political rhetoric of the government of the day, the end result is not all that different.

One of the ways in which the influence of financial markets makes itself felt is through the action of bond-rating agencies, e.g. Moody's or Standard and Poor's, concerned with the creditworthiness of governments and other borrowers. A government whose creditworthiness is downgraded by these international agencies will have to pay higher interest on bonds and indeed, may be shunned by international lenders as a bad risk. The threat of downgrading itself or even putting a government on 'credit watch' can be a powerful signal to mend its ways. In this way national capital, with the backing of international finance, is able to pressurize governments to toe the line.

Sometimes a national government and international bond-rating agencies may have a tacit understanding whereby well-timed warnings on creditworthiness are issued in order to help the government to administer the 'medicine' of programme cuts and reduced spending. This is, roughly speaking, what happened in Canada in 1995 when large spending cuts were implemented by a government elected on a platform of maintaining social programmes. A 'crisis' atmosphere was created around the Canadian economy and its future in order to drive home the 'gravity' of the deficit situation. As Barlow and Campbell describe:

Through the fall of 1994 and the first months of 1995, the deficit scare grew to hurricane force: Axworthy, Martin, and other government spokespersons warned that, if Canada didn't take the hard fiscal medicine, the international financial markets and the International Monetary Fund would force even harder medicine upon us (1995, p. 137).

More significantly the 'chorus in support of deficit slashing was nothing new. What was new was ... that the spectre of international debt terrorism forcing us to our knees had been brought to the top of the political agenda' (ibid.). An editorial in the *Wall Street Journal* warned that if 'dramatic action is not taken in next month's federal budget, Canada could hit the debt wall ... and have to call in the International Monetary Fund' (ibid., p. 139). A few days before the budget, Moody's – a leading credit-rating agency – put the federal government on a credit watch which sent 'shock waves through the markets and the media' (ibid., p. 144).

Opinion polls showed that for the first time, the public had bought heavily into deficit reduction. Soon the budget was passed. The cuts were massive. Even the finance minister acknowledged that it was 'the most radical reduction in government since demobilization from a wartime to a peacetime economy' (ibid., p. 143). A not dissimilar example of a crisis orchestrated as a preliminary to radical reforms is provided by New Zealand in 1984 (Cameron and Finn, 1996, p. 116; Massey, 1995, pp. 69–71).

These examples do not in any way imply that globalization is little more than mythmaking and scare tactics on the part of neoliberals. It is both a 'subjective' and an 'objective' presence in the global economy of the 1990s. It brings outside pressure to bear on national governments and at the same time also helps to insulate government policies from democratic political pressures to act otherwise.

The source of a more general influence on government policy is the importance of 'investor confidence'. How the business community perceives the investment climate of a country is important: in a globalized economy financial investors can decide to take their money out of a country in a matter of minutes, leaving the national currency extremely vulnerable. And although as we have seen (Chapter 2), decisions about industrial investment and location depend on a host of factors, investors – whether domestic or foreign – do have a choice of where to invest. Attracting foreign investment and retaining the confidence of domestic investors is therefore important. Reducing the national debt and deficit, mainly by reducing social spending and keeping a lid on inflation, seem to be major priorities for creating investor confidence. National governments ignore them at their peril.

Quite apart from the constraints of the global market, a strong influence in the same direction is exercised by intergovernmental agencies such as the IMF and OECD (see pp. 8–11). Dealing with debt and deficit is one of the policy matters on which these agencies proffer expert advice to industrialized nations (CCPA, 1996, p. 9; Collier, 1995). Although their influence on rich industrial nations – unlike the ex-communist or Third World nations subject to conditionalities – is usually indirect, it is nonetheless important. Moreover the reports, the assessment of policies and the advice offered by these agencies provide a good deal of ammunition to domestic forces which favour a neoliberal approach to deficits and social spending.

Again, such outside 'expert' opinion helps to insulate governments from democratic pressures to act otherwise. As we saw in the Canadian example above, the idea that if we don't put our financial house in order, it will be done for us by the global market place or agencies such as the IMF can be a powerful argument for reducing the debt and deficit by slashing social expenditure. Regional economic associations such as the EU and NAFTA constitute yet another source of supranational constraint on government policy.

In the case of the EU, the Maastricht Treaty includes some strict monetary and fiscal criteria for membership in the European monetary union. These convergence criteria require that the budget deficit be no more than 3 per cent and the accumulated national debt no more than 60 per cent of GDP. Inflation also has to be kept down within specified limits (European Parliament, 1992, pp. 2–9; Leibfried and Pierson, 1995a, pp. 72–3). Eleven of the 15 members of the EU have qualified to join the monetary union by bringing their deficits within 3 per cent of GDP although in some countries the accumulated debt remains high[2] (OECD, 1998, pp. 34–5; Walker, 1998, p. 18). In the course of this fiscal exercise many countries, including France and Germany, were hard put to meet these criteria as they struggled with their deficits and sought large reductions in social expenditures. In France Maastricht-induced austerity policies led to massive protests, including strikes, and brought a socialist government to power pledged to reverse such policies (Bensaid, 1996; Bowd, 1995).

We shall look at the political response to globalization in the next chapter and at the social policy of supranational organizations in the final chapter. Suffice to note here that the influence of the EU on social protection is two-sided. On the one hand the EU has put in place measures such as the Social Charter, aimed at providing minimum social protection for workers within member countries. On the other hand its policy of fiscal austerity, such as that enshrined in the Maastricht Treaty, works the other way, i.e. towards retrenching social protection in member countries. Moreover, the criterion of 'subsidiarity' endorsed by the EU implies that social policy is largely a matter for national governments rather than for the Community as a whole (Streeck, 1995, p. 426).

FISCAL POLICY

The freedom to tax and spend is perhaps at the heart of the ability of nation states to fashion an autonomous social policy. Advanced welfare states in countries such as Belgium, the Netherlands, Sweden and Denmark have been premised on the freedom of governments to tax and spend in accordance with national preference and priorities expressed through the ballot box. Included in this autonomy of fiscal policy is the principle of progressive taxation, closely associated with the idea of a substantial social state. It appears that globalization is in the process of eroding these basic premises of the KWS.

Once again we find that the neoliberal counter-revolution in taxation which began in earnest with the Thatcher and Reagan administrations, is being carried further forward by globalization. Neoliberals justified the sharp re-duction in taxes on high-income earners chiefly on the grounds that it would provide an incentive for wealth creation and strengthen market forces more generally. In any case the neoliberal philosophy of greater market orientation and less government translated into lower rates of income tax and govern-ment spending generally.

The sharp fall in the rates of taxation on higher incomes in countries such as the US and the UK since the late 1970s is well documented as is the substantial loss of revenue resulting therefrom. (On the US see, for example, Reich, 1992, p. 260 and Greider, 1993, p. 80; for the UK see CSJ, 1994, p. 31.) Other Anglo-Saxon countries have tended to follow in the footsteps of the UK and the US, although the precise nature and extent of change varies. In Continental Europe and Japan too, top rates of taxation have tended to come down, although countries vary a great deal in the nature and extent of tax reform (Sandford, 1993, p. 12; OECD, 1998, pp. 160–62). The deregula-tion of capital and financial markets in the 1980s meant greater mobility of capital and opportunities for investment world-wide. This has provided a further boost to the reduction of top income tax rates and the easing of corporate taxes.

True, thus far we have not seen a 'tax war', i.e. an open competition among countries to reduce taxes in order to lure investment capital. But there is little doubt that low taxation is one of the principal attractions for businesses when considering location or investment in a country, and governments cannot ignore this (Owens, 1993, pp. 24–8). Globalization thus makes for a strong presumption in favour of lowering taxes, especially taxes on high incomes and corporate profits (Sandford, 1993, pp. 220–22). As Tables 3.1 and 3.2 show, over the last decade or so, most OECD countries have reduced the top rates on income as well as corporate taxes.

On average, however, total tax revenue as a percentage of GDP has not come down in OECD countries.[3] The loss of revenue from the reduction of

Table 3.1　Top central government[1] marginal personal tax rates (%) on
earnings (selected OECD countries)

	1980	1986	1992
G7			
Canada	43	34	31.8
France	60	65	56.8
Germany	56	56	55
Italy	72	62	50
Japan	75	70	50
UK	60	60	40
US	70	50	31
Others			
Australia	65[2]	57	48
Austria	62	62	50
Denmark	39.6	45	40
Netherlands	72	72	60
New Zealand	60[2]	57	33
Norway	48	40	13
Sweden	50	50	25

Notes:
[1]　Taxes at local government level can be substantial in some countries.
[2]　1976.

Sources:　Owens, 1993, p. 30; Sandford, 1993, p. 12.

direct taxation has been made up largely through the use of indirect taxes,
especially consumption taxes such as the value added tax or the goods and
services tax, as well as higher social insurance contributions and charges
(Sandford, 1993, pp. 14, 20; OECD, 1998, pp. 159–62; on New Zealand see
Stephens, 1993, pp. 47–9). Some of these, such as higher payroll taxes or
employers' contributions, have also come under criticism for creating a disin-
centive to hiring workers.

In most countries tax reform has shifted the burden downwards to the
middle- and low-income population while providing high-income earners
with large tax breaks. Thus financing for public expenditure has been sustained in part through borrowing, resulting in higher deficits and in part by
maintaining overall taxation levels but shifting to regressive taxation (OECD,
1998, 159–62). Once again these trends – including tax regressivity – are
more pronounced in Anglo-Saxon countries, although the general direction of

Table 3.2　Overall (national and local) corporate tax rates (%) (selected OECD countries)

	1980	1986	1992
G7			
Canada	42.4	51.6	43.5[1]
France	50	50	34
Germany	61.7/44.3[2]	61.7/44.3	58.6/46.0
Italy	36.3	47.8/36.0	47.8/36.0
Japan	52/42	55.4/45.4	50
UK	52	40	33
US	49.2	49.5	38.3
Others			
Austria	61.5/38.3	61.5/38.3	39
Denmark	37	50	38
Netherlands	46	42	35
Sweden	40	52	30

Notes:
[1]　38% for manufacturing industry.
[2]　Where two rates are given the first is on retentions, the second on distributions.

Source:　Owens, 1993, p. 35.

the change appears to be the same in almost all countries (ibid.). The ascendancy of neoliberal ideology reinforced by globalization pressures has tended to delegitimize progressive taxation and changed the ideological climate very much in favour of reducing direct taxation all round.

A part of this ideology is the notion that economic activity, including spending, should be privatized as far as possible. People should be free to keep and to spend as much of their income as possible themselves. Finally, we should note once again that international agencies such as the IMF and the OECD have been actively promoting tax reforms along the lines sketched above. Similarly, the EU has been involved in the promotion of consumption taxes, e.g. the VAT (value added tax) in member countries (Sandford, 1993, p. 20).

The delegitimation of progressive taxation and the growth of tax regressivity has a number of consequences. First, it means that taxes and transfers taken together do much less to redistribute incomes downwards. Indeed as we saw in the previous chapter income inequality – both before and after taxes – in most English-speaking countries has increased sharply, with tax regressivity contributing to the vast redistribution of income upwards. Secondly, the point made by Reich (1992, p. 250) in relation to the US has wider validity, namely that most ordinary working citizens 'cannot afford to shoulder the added financial burden of higher levels of public spending'. Third, there seems to be a ratchet effect at work as far as direct taxation is concerned. Once direct taxes are lowered, it may be difficult politically to raise them again.

THE SHRINKING TAX BASE

The growth of MNCs and the increasing internationalization of the production of goods and services is having a deleterious effect on government revenues. About one-third of world trade (the proportion can be higher for individual countries, e.g. for the US it is half of the total trade by value) is now intrafirm trade, i.e. transfers among constituent parts of the same MNC (UN, 1994, p. 10; Reich, 1992, p. 114). The price at which these goods are 'sold' or transferred is not determined by the market but by the MNC itself.

Now these transfer prices can be adjusted in such a way as to minimize the profit or indeed, show a loss in a high-tax country and profit in a country where corporate taxes are low or non-existent. The mechanism of 'transfer pricing' provides MNCs with plenty of scope for tax avoidance. Little is known about the extent of revenue lost through transfer pricing.

A recent study (1990) of the US Congress found that more than half of about 40 foreign firms surveyed had paid virtually no taxes over a ten–year period (Dicken, 1992, p. 391). In 1987, a boom year, it was found that 59 per cent of foreign corporations reported no profits in the US and paid no tax. Over the last three years their revenue had gone up by 50 per cent but taxes paid by only 2 per cent (Barnet and Kavanagh, 1994, p. 345). Clearly multinationalization of production is providing corporations with plenty of opportunity for tax avoidance.

Cash-strapped governments are trying to do something about all this. For example, in the US the state government of California 'grew tired of multinationals active in the state moving their profits elsewhere' (Drohan, 1994, p. B6) and decided that companies must pay tax based on a proportion of their world-wide earnings. But this ruling is being contested in the courts. According to a study by Australian tax authorities 'billions of dollars' are being lost in revenue to MNCs. Deductions for interest payments and transfer pricing policies account for most of the revenue loss in Australia. Thus during 1993–4, 60 per cent of the MNCs (both foreign and Australian) claimed to have made no profits and paid no taxes (CCPA, 1997, p. 3).

A recent move by the US government to levy substantial fines on companies which do not account properly for their internal cross-border transactions has prompted the Canadian government to propose tighter measures to ensure that 'multinational corporations don't shift profits out of the country to avoid paying taxes in Canada' (McCarthy, 1997, p. B7). In Germany an attempt to impose a withholding tax on interest paid to residents resulted in a massive outflow of funds to neighbouring Luxembourg (Owens, 1993, p. 31). Indeed with the ease of transferring funds from one country to another, a substantial amount of investment is now taking place overseas, including tax havens.

All of these developments contribute, perhaps substantially, to the erosion of the tax base. While national governments are aware of the issues involved and the OECD has been studying aspects of taxation for some time, nothing concrete has emerged so far. Apparently the governments of OECD countries have 'shown no appetite to address the broader question of what globalization is doing to the overall integrity of their tax bases' (Drohan, 1994, p. B6).

A further drain on national revenue results from the tendency of corporations – domestic and foreign – to extract substantial concessions in the form of tax holidays, subsidies, write-offs and the like from governments. The point is that as the state withdraws from productive and job-creating activities, countries have to rely on private capital for economic development and job creation. Here the MNCs, because they have a choice to invest wherever they like, are able to extract substantial financial aid from governments. The amounts get higher as the bidding becomes more competitive.

In 1977, for example, the state of Ohio in the US 'induced Honda to build its auto plant there by promising $22 million in subsidies and tax breaks: by 1986 it took a $100 m. package from Kentucky for Toyota to create about the same number of jobs there' (Reich, 1992, p. 296). When in 1985 Mitsubishi announced that it would begin assembling automobiles in America, four states competed for the plant. The 'winner' was Illinois, with a ten-year package of $276 m. in incentives and direct aid costing about $25 000 a year for each new job to be created.

Such incentives are apparently 'becoming ever more generous' (Reich, 1992, p. 296). More recent studies of investment patterns concur. According to a recent report of the UN (1995, p. xliii), competition for foreign direct investment has 'led more and more governments to offer increasingly generous incentives to influence the locational decisions' and the 'number and range of incentive programmes available to foreign investors has increased over the past ten years'.

ERODING SOCIAL CITIZENSHIP

The pressure on governments to reduce the deficit and debt and to lower taxes translates into reduced social spending. The result is a weakening, if not erosion, of the second line of defence erected by the KWS, in the form of institutions of social citizenship, against poverty, social exclusion and dependency. The pace of change varies and the erosion is speedier under neoconservative governments. Moreover, as we have emphasized all along, it is in Anglo-Saxon countries that we are seeing the most dramatic changes. Nonetheless in Western Europe and Japan, too, the trends are not dissimilar (see Chapter 5 for details). Considerations of international competitiveness, the dominance of the Anglo-Saxon neoliberal model in international decision-making, the greater openness of economies and increasing mobility of capital are creating similar pressures for change.

Retrenching Social Security

One aspect of the erosion of social citizenship is the retreat from universality, a basic principle underlying the KWS. While in some countries universality is being compromised and eroded, in others it is being scaled back quite substantially. Of the two major social programmes of the welfare state, income security and health care, it is in the former that the retreat from universality is more evident.

As the resources available to the social state shrink, the argument that higher-income groups can look after themselves becomes more appealing. Conversely, the wisdom of the notion that when resources are scarce, they should be used to help the needy rather than lavished indiscriminately on all citizens, is only too obvious. What neoliberalism presents as ideology, globalization makes into a virtue and a necessity. Thus the ground is prepared for moving income security systems from a universal to a selective basis.

The first casualties of the assault on universality have been the non-contributory income security programmes financed out of general revenue ('demogrants'), which paid benefits, e.g. family allowances and old age pensions, to all citizens irrespective of income. These programmes are being subjected to a taxback for higher-income beneficiaries on the road to becoming income- or means-tested (see for example *The Economist*, 1995; Stephens, 1996, p. 55; Castles, 1996, pp. 106–8; Myles, 1996, pp. 126, 136). Although contributory insurance programmes generally retain universal coverage, they are being subjected to a variety of restrictions and cutbacks, e.g. reduced benefits and stricter entitlement (see for example Clasen and Gould, 1995, pp. 193, 196; Stephens, 1996, pp. 45–6; Taylor-Gooby, 1996b, p. 210). In some countries they are being privatized, e.g. in the UK, sickness benefits were made a responsibility of employers (Taylor-Gooby, 1996a, pp. 105–6).

One programme that has suffered savage cuts in a number of countries, e.g. the US, the UK and Canada, is unemployment insurance (on the US and the UK see Pierson, 1994, pp. 106–7, 119–20; on Canada see Battle, 1997, pp. 17–22, 40; on the UK see Sinfield, 1994, p. 132). This has to do in part with the ideology of labour market 'flexibility' which sees unemployment benefits as a source of 'rigidity' and 'distortion', creating 'disincentives' for job searches and mobility and preventing wages from going down. In short unemployment compensation is seen as causing unemployment. Thus reduction, even if not elimination, of benefits for the able-bodied unemployed is seen as a necessary condition for job creation in the private sector.

Social assistance or 'welfare' is seen as presenting similar problems. With long-term unemployment on the rise, the number of people on social assistance has been growing. In the case of the able-bodied on assistance, namely the unemployed and sole support mothers, there is once again the perceived 'problem' of disincentives and welfare dependency. Moreover, the cost of social assistance has tended to rise. As a response to these developments there is pressure to reduce the level of benefits and impose stricter conditions of eligibility for the able-bodied. The latter includes some form of work or training as a condition for receiving social assistance. In essence this is what 'workfare' is about; an approach to social assistance which came into being in the United States during the Reagan presidency (see for example Burghes, 1990; Pierson, 1994, pp. 122–3). The Clinton administration has taken it further in that social assistance to the able-bodied has been made conditional on 'work' in some form and its duration strictly limited (Morley and Petras, 1998, p. 129).[4] While the US must have pride of place as the initiator of 'workfare', in some form or other the idea has since been taken up by other countries. The restructuring of income security programmes for the unemployed is related to the 'flexibilization' and recommodification of the labour market as outlined in the previous chapter.

The *principle* of universal coverage and equality of access remains more resistant to erosion in the case of medical care. No doubt this is largely because of the strong support it receives from the vast majority of the population. But it would be a mistake to assume that it cannot be whittled down incrementally. Thus here too we see higher charges and fees, reduced services, a decline in the quality of services and privatization. Since a direct assault on the principle of universal medical care is hazardous politically, governments are employing indirect methods for reaching the same broad objectives.

For example the Canadian government has resorted to a stratagem known as 'social policy by stealth'. While endorsing the *principle* of universality and equality of access in medical care, the federal government resorts to massive funding cutbacks in order to reduce social spending and balance the books. Ostensibly this shifts the responsibility for funding to the provincial level of government, but in effect it means the erosion of medical services.

Let us look at some examples of trends in income security in English-speaking countries since the late 1970s. In the UK there has been a marked shift towards selectivity. The population on means-tested assistance rose from 4.4 million in 1979 to 8.2 million in 1988 (Johnson, 1990, p. 47). Spending on means-tested assistance doubled between 1978 and 1994, rising to 34 per cent of all social spending (*The Economist*, 1995, p. 23; Sinfield, 1994, p. 139). How far-reaching the change has been can be gauged from the fact that in 1995 nearly half of British households were said to have at least one person receiving a means-tested benefit (Field, 1995).

In New Zealand the period since the mid-1980s has seen a shift towards targeting and stricter eligibility for benefits with the major changes coming, under a neoliberal government, after 1990. The move towards privatization and economic liberalization began under a Labour government while re-trenchment of the social sector followed later under a right-wing government. In the name of reducing the budget deficit and making New Zealand more competitive, the social safety net has been virtually shredded (Kelsey, 1995; Boston, 1993).

Changes since the mid-1980s include the following: the universal family benefit was abolished; eligibility for income or means-tested programmes such as unemployment, sickness and widowhood has been tightened consid-erably and the level of benefits reduced, resulting in up to 30 per cent reduction in benefits for the unemployed. Universal retirement pensions have become subject to a 25 per cent surcharge for higher income seniors and the age of retirement is to rise from 60 to 65 by 2001 (Boston, 1993, pp. 69–71; Kelsey, 1995, p. 276).

The direction of change in Canada has been similar. Universal family allowance became subject to a taxback in 1989 and was replaced by income-tested family benefits in 1993. The universal old age pension became subject to a taxback (as in New Zealand) in 1989. Eligibility as well as the level of unemployment insurance benefits have been cut repeatedly in recent years. These cuts, together with longer spells of unemployment, have resulted in a drop in the percentage of unemployed receiving benefits from 87 per cent in 1989 to nearly 40 per cent in 1997. Drastic reductions in federal funding for health, higher education and social assistance and the downloading of re-sponsibility to the provinces has severely compromised the universal medicare scheme. The federal Canada Assistance Plan, which helped to maintain mini-mum national standards of social assistance across Canada, has been abolished (Barlow and Campbell, 1995, pp. 148–55).

Overall these changes have been justified by the need to reduce the deficit and debt and to create a more congenial climate for private sector investment and enterprise. They are also a part of the strategy of divesting federal responsibility for social programmes and devolving responsibility to the prov-inces. Again politics seem to matter little. The retreat from universality and the withdrawal of the federal government from commitment to a national minimum had begun under a Conservative administration. The policy has been carried forward and intensified by Liberals, the erstwhile architects of the Canadian welfare state (Barlow and Campbell, 1995, Chapters 5 and 6).

Indeed Canada's spectacular success in shrinking the budget deficit (and later turning it into a surplus) by a massive reduction in social spending has not gone unnoticed internationally. According to one commentator, Canada has transformed itself into 'one of the leanest public economies in the developed world' with Chretien, the Liberal Prime Minister leading 'the budget cutting, with more success than nearly any other Western leader' (Swardson, 1996, p. 17).

In the United States, too, the budget deficit has been reduced quite substantially in recent years and has now been eliminated. But this owes more to an economic upturn and higher revenues than to a reduction in social expenditures, although the latter has also played a part. Interestingly, the US shows far less of a move from universal to selective programmes, in part because it had few universal programmes to cut, except the insurance-based 'social security', i.e. retirement and disability pensions. Unlike Canada, the US did not have either family allowances or old age pensions, two universal non-contributory programmes one of which has now been abolished in Canada. Social Security, a contributory and thus an entitlement programme for the aged, has been highly resistant to change (Pierson, 1994, p. 69; Day, 1990, pp. 33, 80, 99–100).

A good deal of attention in the US has focused on 'welfare', i.e. AFDC and other social assistance programmes, and it is these means-tested programmes that have been more vulnerable to cutbacks (Mishra, 1990, pp. 25, 28; Myles, 1996, p. 135). However, the unemployment insurance programme in the US, never really very generous, has been substantially retrenched (Pierson, 1994, pp. 119–20). Medicare or the health insurance programme for the aged, has also suffered cutbacks (ibid., pp. 137–8) and more far-reaching changes in social security and medical care, i.e. to move these towards private provision, have been proposed quite recently (Myles, 1996, p. 135).

The specifics of policy retrenchment vary from one country to another depending on a host of national factors. For example in the US, the targeting of 'welfare', i.e. AFDC, cannot be understood in isolation from the issue of race. The US is also somewhat exceptional in that a comparatively large military expenditure provides an alternative to scaling back civilian expenditure as a means of deficit reduction. There are, of course, a variety of factors which influence retrenchment of social programmes, including the nature of political institutions, the structure of the income security system and policy feedback. Globalization is important in setting the broader economic and ideological context within which policy decisions occur, but its influence is mediated through the political economy of the nation state (see Chapters 4 and 5). The following chapter will explore in some detail the influence of democratic politics in counteracting the pressures of globalization and neoliberalism.

No doubt, even in Anglo-Saxon countries a substantial part of the structure of social provision remains in place. Moreover, social expenditure as a percentage of GNP has not decreased in most countries. However, the expenditure data must be treated with caution. For as we have seen in Chapter 2, the recommodification of the labour market – in terms of chronic unemployment, low wages and insecure employment – means that a larger social expenditure is necessary to maintain minimum standards. For example the much-vaunted Earned Income Tax Credit in the US is undoubtedly helping the working poor. But it has been necessary because of the vast growth in low-wage employment. Thus it has to be seen as a modern form of the 'Speenhamland' system, a state subsidy to employers of low-wage labour.

Any realistic assessment of today's social expenditure must take into account the increased outlay necessary to compensate for the 'diswelfare' created by globalization and a 'post-Fordist' labour market. It must also be remembered that unemployment, for example, not only creates an economic problem but also a variety of social problems such as family violence, alcoholism, depression and illness, which involve additional social expenditure. When these 'diswelfare' costs are taken into account, effective social expenditure is likely to be a good deal lower than nominal expenditure as a percentage of GDP would suggest.

The question posed at the beginning of this chapter was that with the first line of defence against insecurity and deprivation erected by the KWS, i.e. full employment and good wages having been undermined by globalization, whether the second line of defence, i.e. institutionalized social rights, was being strengthened or at least maintained. We have argued that in the context of globalization, the second line of defence is under considerable pressure, if not under attack, and has eroded a good deal in some countries.

It appears that through a globalized economy, pressures for 'competitive austerity' are becoming institutionalized in industrial nations. Income security programmes directly related to the recommodification of the labour market, notably unemployment insurance and social assistance to the able-bodied, are under assault as are tax-financed universal programmes. More indirectly, social expenditures are under pressure through a variety of policies legitimated with reference to competitiveness and other globalization issues. These include reduction of the deficit and debt and the reduction of taxes, including payroll taxes.

True, neoliberal governments seem to be pursuing this course far more aggressively than governments of a centrist or leftist persuasion. Moreover Anglo-Saxon countries are much further advanced along this road. There is little direct evidence of social dumping in the sense of capital moving out of countries with a high level of social protection. Nonetheless the presumption of investor-friendly policies suggests the potential for further downward pressure on social protection. In sum it appears that the current is flowing strongly in one direction and that by design or default, social citizenship is in the process of eroding.

SUMMARY AND CONCLUSIONS

The changes outlined in this and the previous chapter concerning the economy, the labour market and social protection translate into a growing social deficit. Whereas living standards rose steadily in Western countries during the golden age (c.1950–75) and poverty declined, largely as a result of social intervention, this trend has been halted since the late 1970s.

As might be expected the situation is worse in Anglo-Saxon countries, with the UK, the US and New Zealand in the forefront. In these countries globalization and strong neoliberal tendencies in policy-making have come together to erode social citizenship and to weaken, if not repudiate, the earlier commitment to a social minimum as of right. Labour market restructuring, deregulation and taxation policies have combined to create substantial inequalities of income and wealth distribution.[5]

True, selective policies have been employed to good effect, for example in Canada. In Australia and New Zealand relatively generous means-tested programmes have been a key feature of income security for a long time. Moreover, the use of income-testing, as distinct from means-testing typical of social assistance programmes is able to overcome the problem of stigma and take-up to a large degree. In the US the Earned Income Tax Credit, expanded substantially in recent years, is helping the working poor.

It should, however, be remembered that targeting and selectivity give rise to problems of poverty trap and disincentives to work or save. Benefits therefore have to be kept low, especially for the working-age population, thus limiting the potential for poverty alleviation. At any rate judging by changes in income security programmes, Anglo-Saxon countries are moving away from an institutional to a residual conception of social welfare. What began earlier as a *national* project under neoconservative governments has now become generalized as part of the economic agenda of globalization. Overall, however, ad hoc adjustments, reactive changes to fiscal pressures or other exigencies and political counter-pressures are often leaving systems of social protection in a state of pragmatic indeterminacy.

How are citizens in capitalist democracies responding to these developments? And what are the sources of resistance to globalization pressures and the erosion of social protection? These are the major concerns of the following chapter.

NOTES

1. For example in Canada, 50 per cent of the increase in deficit between 1975/76 and 1988/89 was due to revenue shortfall relative to GDP, 44 per cent to increase in debt charges relative to GDP and only 6 per cent to higher programme spending relative to GDP (McBride and Shields, 1997, p. 58).
2. Some member countries have had to resort to 'creative accounting' in order to meet the 3 per cent deficit criterion. Although the EU regulations leave room for flexibility, members of the EMU are expected to meet the Maastricht targets and maintain strict fiscal discipline (Walker, 1998, p. 18).
3. Tax revenue (including social security contributions) in the OECD area rose from 35 per cent of GDP in 1980 to 38 per cent in 1990 and 38.7 per cent in 1993. Significantly, the percentage declined in all Anglo-Saxon countries between 1990 and 1993 and also in some high-tax countries such as Sweden where it dropped from 55.6 to 49.9 per cent of GDP (OECD 1995d, p. 73, Table 3).
4. In 1996 the AFDC programme or 'welfare' was replaced by the Temporary Assistance for Needy Families programme. There is a five-year lifetime limit on receiving this benefit. Adults are required to begin 'work' (employment, community service, education or training) within two years of receiving assistance. The law delegates much of the programme design to the states (OECD, 1996b, p. 103).
5. It is perhaps symptomatic of the times that the report of the CSJ (1994) on Britain, which may be seen as laying out New Labour's approach to social questions, makes no reference at all to the distribution of wealth, even though it explores inequality of income as well as other forms of inequality in some detail. The influential book by Will Hutton (1995a) on the state of Britain devotes a chapter to inequality, but once again, scarcely mentions wealth. It would appear that inequality of wealth has gone off the political agenda of the Centre Left, no doubt because it raises the spectre of progressive taxation. Income inequality is still on the agenda, in part because of its relevance to social programmes but also because education and training are supposed to reduce the wage gap. Increasingly, the literature on social policy and the welfare state has also been concerned with the politics of 'difference', that is with social rather than economic inequities. On the distribution of income and wealth in the UK see Hills (1995).

4. Social policy and democracy: do politics still matter?

Chapter 2 outlined the consequences of globalization for the economy and the labour market. Chapter 3 looked at the implications of globalization for social policy and found that changes in social protection have been working in the same direction as economic changes. Focusing on Anglo-Saxon countries, we found that the social safety net is weakening, social standards are spiralling downwards and there is a steep rise in inequality. With chronic unemployment, greater economic insecurity and low wages, household incomes are under downward pressure. This chapter looks at the political response to these developments at the nation-state level – more specifically at the role of democracy in preventing the erosion of the welfare state.

Few would disagree with the view that the welfare state is largely a product of mass democracy and electoral competition. Social policy therefore is a matter of political choice. Put simply, political parties compete for office on the basis of different policy platforms and if elected, proceed to implement their particular brand of policy. In English-speaking countries this has generally taken the form of a competition among conservative (right), liberal (centre) and social democratic (left) parties. Indeed, reacting against the explanations of the welfare state based on theories of technological and economic determinism prevalent in the 1960s, a 'politics matter' school emerged in the late 1970s which drew attention to the influence of democratic politics on social policy (Castles, 1982). In particular political scientists singled out social democratic governance and working-class mobilization as potent influences, both quantitative and qualitative, on the development of the welfare state (Korpi, 1983; Esping-Andersen, 1985).

Some went so far as to see the potential of system transformation, i.e. a transition from capitalism to socialism through the welfare state and other reforms (Stephens, 1979). Moreover, in the wake of the neoconservative assault on the welfare state, political scientists of widely divergent persuasions argued that institutions of social protection were deeply entrenched in capitalist democracies and could not be undone short of the abolition of democracy itself. Not only would electoral considerations protect the social safety net from erosion, but organized interests and lobbies would also see to it that programmes which benefited them could not be retrenched. These considerations led to the widespread belief that the welfare state had become an irreversible part of the political economy of advanced capitalist societies and that only minor changes and impairments were likely (Mishra, 1990, pp. 32–3; Pierson, 1994).

True, the experience of the last couple of decades suggests that despite a great deal of neoconservative rhetoric about rolling back the welfare state, the results have so far been modest. Commitment to full employment has been abandoned (with the tacit acceptance of the inevitability of unemployment) and this is a major break with the KWS, at least as it developed in Europe and Australasia. However, mainstream social programmes, including unemployment insurance, remain in place albeit with impairments and cutbacks. No doubt this is largely because of democratic institutions. In the *absence* of electoral democracy and associated political rights and the activity of interest groups and social movements in protecting social programmes, changes would have been far more drastic. This led many commentators to believe that the so-called 'crisis' of the welfare state was now behind us and that the neoconservative assault on the welfare state, in so far as there was one, had been beaten back. Further growth in social programmes and benefits was not to be expected, but neither should we expect substantial cutbacks. The welfare state, it was argued, had reached a state of 'stability' and 'maturity' and what was now needed was a prudent and efficient management of this sector (see Mishra, 1990, pp. 106–8).

Elsewhere I have expressed my doubts and reservations about this 'optimistic' stable state scenario (ibid.). Here I wish to argue that if this viewpoint – which predates globalization – did have some validity earlier, it has even less now. The main reason is that globalization has altered this scenario of stability in quite fundamental ways, furnishing a strong new rationale for the retrenchment of the welfare state.

How valid is this assertion? The rest of this chapter is an attempt to answer this question in light of the arguments of political pluralists and the 'politics matter' school of social scientists.

PARTY COMPETITION AND SOCIAL POLICY

It would be absurd to deny the influence of democratic politics on social welfare policies. Whether there is a conservative, liberal or social democratic government in office matters. What seems to have happened, however, is a substantial narrowing of the choices available to the parties of the Left by way of fiscal and monetary policies and social expenditure (Taylor-Gooby, 1996b, pp. 214–15; George, 1998, p. 28).

We saw in Chapter 2 that Keynesian strategies of maintaining full employment are not working any longer and there is a rise in chronic unemployment everywhere. Moreover the 'tax and spend' policies of advanced social democracies, in short distributive socialism, are now faced with the pressures stemming from globalization identified in the previous chapter. These include reducing debt and deficit through cutting back social spending, lowering levels of taxation and replacing universality with targeting and privatization. To these we might add pressures for deregulation with obvious implications for the weakening, if not abolition of programmes of affirmative action, pay equity and the like.

Not surprisingly, liberal and social democratic parties are drifting closer to their right-wing counterparts in terms of policies, even if not in rhetoric (George, 1998, p. 28). Earlier policy options of social democracy, e.g. nationalization and the public ownership of industries, redistributive and progressive taxation, and job creation through public sector expansion, have virtually disappeared. At best social democracy is striving to slow down the erosion of social protection and to ensure a more equitable process of retrenchment, i.e. one which protects the weaker and more vulnerable population. Overall, thanks to democratic institutions and electoral considerations, change has been and is likely to be gradual and incremental. Yet the *direction* of change is also clear. Simplifying somewhat, we might say that governments of the Left find themselves in a position of reluctant neoliberalism while at the other end of the ideological spectrum neoconservative governments pursue an agenda of retrenchment and privatization of social protection with a great deal of élan.

Indeed in this respect the situation in the 1990s is almost the reverse of that of the 1960s, the heyday of the KWS. At that time social policy converged on a centre-left position with virtually all governments – notwithstanding their ideological billing – more or less implementing the welfare state agenda of full employment or something close to it and willy-nilly following a policy of extending and consolidating a system of social protection.

Today social policy is converging on a right-of-centre position with global capitalism driving policy rightwards (George, 1998). Again the situation today is the obverse of that of the golden age of welfare capitalism. At that time social programmes and expenditures were spiralling upwards with seemingly no logical ceiling to levels of taxation and public spending. Today they are drifting downwards and once again with apparently no rationale or limit to the downsizing of social programmes. True, the golden age saw an explosive growth of social rights in most Western countries, and West European countries in particular are the inheritors of sizeable welfare states. With the notable exception of the UK, we see only modest changes so far by way of the residualization and downsizing of social welfare in these countries.

Are they then immune to the pressures of globalization? This question of cross-national differences in response to globalization and their implications is one which we shall take up in the next chapter. What is important to note here is the fact that what we are witnessing is more a difference in social policy *between nation states* than between political parties. Thus it is not so much politics as the political economy of nation states that seems to matter today.

At any rate as far as Anglo-Saxon countries are concerned, it seems clear that parties of the Centre or Left find it difficult to offer social policies that are sufficiently distinguished from those on offer from the Right.[1] Whereas the radical Right pursues a clearly inegalitarian policy of welfare retrenchment with scant regard for fairness and equity, social democrats and liberals follow the path of 'progressive' austerity.[2] All the same, the idea of the 'affordable' welfare state seems to have become a point of convergence (George and Miller, 1994).

The lack of alternatives and choice is leading to a sense of disenchantment with democratic politics. Citizens are likely to find that no matter which party they elect, social welfare policies tend to be dictated by financial markets, MNCs, and supranational organizations which lack accountability. Yet political parties, especially those of the centre or left persuasion, are likely to campaign on a platform that promises a set of policies different from those of the Right. When in office therefore, politicians are hard put to defend policies which are the opposite of what they promised when campaigning.

The result is an increasing amount of doublespeak causing disillusion and disenchantment with politics. The liberal government in Canada, elected in 1993, is a case in point (Barlow and Campbell, 1995). The Chirac presidency in France prior to the election of L. Jospin is another example (*Guardian Weekly*, 1995; Bowd, 1995, p. 94). On the other hand if centre or left parties campaign on a platform which differs little from that of the Right, that too leads to a feeling that there is no choice. It is important, of course, to remember that we are thinking here of welfare state policies alone. It goes without saying that in many other areas of policy as well as in matters of administration and style of governance, party politics matter. The Labour Government of Tony Blair in Britain is a case in point.

In some English-speaking countries the electorate has responded by turning to third parties. The simple majority system of elections in English-speaking countries encourages a two-party system; the turn to the third party comes out of the electorate's sense of a lack of choice. For example in the presidential election in the United States in 1992, close to 1 in 5 Americans voted for the independent candidate Ross Perot (Gold, 1995, p. 751; Cloud, 1992, p. 49).

Another response to the feeling that major parties are following the same policy agenda has been to move to a system of proportional representation (Mulgan, 1995; Temple, 1995). The shock of the right turn by the Labour

Party in New Zealand, following the 1984 election, was so great as to result in a referendum in which a majority voted in favour of proportional representation. The 1996 election was held on the basis of the new system, resulting in a coalition government. It is too early, however, to say what difference, if any, the new and somewhat complicated system of voting will make to social policy. Since the citizenry still looks to the government (where else could it turn?) as the guardian of the national interest and as representative of the national community, there is a presumption that national governments can and should deliver. Yet at the same time it is also becoming clear that a change of government may do little to solve some of the major problems people face, e.g. persistent unemployment, declining or stagnant incomes and the declining scope and standard of social protection.

However, apart from party politics there are other elements of democracy, notably public opinion and attitudes, interest groups and social movements. To what extent are they able to act as a countervailing force against the erosion of social protection?

PUBLIC OPINION AND ATTITUDES TO WELFARE

Public opinion in Western industrial countries remains overwhelmingly in favour of collective, i.e. government, responsibility for ensuring the well-being of citizens. For example in 1990 data from six European countries showed that 98 per cent of respondents wanted governments to provide health care, 98 per cent to provide for the elderly, 85 per cent for the unemployed, 75 per cent to provide jobs and 74 per cent to reduce income differences. Despite some fluctuation, overall these attitudes show remarkable consistency over the last twenty-five years or so (Huseby, 1995, pp. 94–6).

A survey of seven major European countries shows 'sweeping majorities in favour of government responsibility for welfare concerns such as old age pensions, medical care, health, and unemployment in both 1974 and 1990' (ibid., p. 95). Although support varies for different programmes and policies, overall attitudes are 'evidently very favourable towards big government: There are clearly many things people want their governments to do' (ibid., p. 94). Although *general* questions about government and taxation often show a preference for smaller government and lower taxes, when it comes to specific issues, e.g. health care, education or pensions, a substantial majority not only want government to be involved but express a willingness to pay higher taxes in order to maintain or improve services.

A superficial reading of the situation suggests that public attitudes are contradictory and that people seem to want to have their cake and eat it too. No doubt people generally prefer lower taxes (or indeed none at all) and this may in part be the reason for the perception that taxes cannot be raised and that for a political party to declare that it is in favour of raising taxes is 'tantamount to electoral suicide' (George, 1996, p. 17).

In fact the issue of taxation is rather complex. Left-wing parties have traditionally favoured, at least in principle, progressive taxation as a basis for equity and fairness. However, given the pressures stemming from globalization as well as the prevalent bias towards neoliberal economics, taxing the rich and corporations is virtually ruled out. And as we saw in the last chapter, neoconservative regimes have shifted the burden of taxation downwards through raising indirect taxes and social security contributions, while sharply reducing the incidence of taxation on higher incomes. The question of tax fairness is therefore an important context within which to evaluate attitudes towards taxation (Greider, 1993, p. 85; Steinmo, 1994, p. 13). In recent years the incomes of many average wage and salary earners have been stagnant or even falling (as in the US and to a lesser extent in Canada), whereas incomes of the rich have been rising and the amount they pay in taxes has been declining. In these circumstances it is not surprising that adding to the existing tax burden is not likely to be popular.

Once again opinion polls show that a large majority of people support the principle of progressive taxation and a substantial majority think the tax burden is unfair with high-income earners being taxed lightly (Confalonieri and Newton, 1995). What attitude surveys reveal is a sign of tax protest, not tax revolt. Public attitudes turn out to be far more rational and consistent when seen in the context of tax fairness and a trade-off between taxation and the provision of services (ibid., p. 142–3). Much of the above evidence comes from Western Europe, including Britain. And it appears that in Britain, support for state welfare and willingness to pay taxes for social services *rose* across the Thatcher years (Timmins, 1994, p. 7). Surveys of North American, especially US, attitudes seem to vary somewhat in their findings but carefully phrased and specific questions about state welfare show a large majority in favour of government responsibility (Cook and Barrett, 1992). A national sample survey of this kind, for example, found that at least 75 per cent of the American public wanted seven main social programmes to be maintained or enhanced and the percentage rose to 96 per cent in the case of Social Security, Medicare and Supplemental Security Income. Moreover the majority of respondents who thought benefits should be increased also expressed willingness to pay higher taxes for the purpose (ibid., pp. 61–65).

Indeed Peter Taylor-Gooby (1994, p. 17), an eminent authority on attitudes to social welfare, finds the notion that 'tax increases are electoral suicide' a 'misconception'. The heavily ideological nature of the belief that the electorate is groaning under the crushing burden of taxation becomes clear when we note that these views are usually expressed by elites, especially in English-speaking countries, whose levels of taxation are relatively light. On the other hand there is virtually no evidence of tax revolt in Continental Europe, where the general level of taxation is much higher but is accepted as necessary in order to finance quality social services.

Yet the stubborn fact remains that despite overwhelming evidence of popular support for social programmes and the willingness to pay taxes for their improvement, these preferences are being set aside on grounds of economic exigency, namely that such democratic preferences are not 'affordable'. Instead the economic orthodoxy in Anglo-Saxon countries prefers to retrench social expenditure and reduce taxes. Private spending is the preferred means of stimulating the economy and combating the recessionary tendencies generated as a result of public sector retrenchment.

Although economic orthodoxy downplays public opinion on the welfare state, the latter has undoubtedly acted as a counterweight to the neoliberal agenda of retrenching social programmes. Governments have had to temper their agenda of cutbacks and resort to social policy 'by stealth', as for example in Canada in the 1980s (Gray, 1990). More recently, however, globalization has provided a strong legitimation for social retrenchment on the basis of international competition and the global market's preference for lower taxes and social spending, thus devaluing public opinion and democratic choice further (Barlow and Campbell, 1995).[3] At any rate this would seem to be the situation, by and large, in Anglo-Saxon countries.

INTEREST GROUPS AND SOCIAL MOVEMENTS

Organized Labour

The labour movement in general and labour unions in particular must be counted among the most important interest groups seeking to influence policy. Indeed organized labour wields considerable power by virtue of its strategic location in the system of production as well as its capacity to support political parties – financially, electorally and in other ways – which would further labour's interests.

Historically organized labour has lent its support to social democratic and other left parties who have been more supportive of the welfare state. Moreover, in many countries organized labour has played a key role in societal decision-making in the post-WW2 years through corporatist institutions. Typically this took the form of tripartite and consensual forms of decision-making involving peak associations of the state, employers and workers. These arrangements – reflecting the strategic position of organized labour in the economy as one of the 'social partners' – were commonplace in many European countries during the golden age of welfare capitalism. This corporatist approach helped to maintain full employment, curb inflation, enhance productivity and sustain or improve social programmes (Mishra, 1984, Chapter 4; Pekkarinen et al., 1992). Unions sought to deliver wage moderation, industrial peace and workers' co-operation in enhancing competitiveness and productivity. In turn the state and employers agreed to the policy of maintaining employment and domestic investment as well as the system of social protection as a quid pro quo.

Indeed seen in historical perspective the labour movement, directly or indirectly, has been a major player in promoting and defending the welfare state (Stephens, 1979; Korpi, 1983; Hicks et al., 1995). What role is it playing now in the defence of social programmes and what has been the impact of globalization on labour's position in society?

While organized labour remains an important interest group, it has seen its power and influence decline since the early 1980s. Conditions naturally vary from one country to another and from one part of the world to another. In most advanced welfare states in Western Europe, organized labour remains a force to be reckoned with despite some decline in membership (OECD, 1997c, p. 71; OECD, 1994c, p. 10, Table 5.8) and the weakening of the institutions of social partnership (Huber and Stephens, 1998). In a number of English-speaking countries, however, notably the UK, the US and New Zealand, organized labour has suffered a serious setback, if not the prospect of emasculation.[4]

Overall organized labour has seen its power and influence weaken for a number of reasons. First, the onset of chronic unemployment and job insecurity has weakened its bargaining power. Secondly, given unemployment and the weaker bargaining power of labour, business no longer needs its co-operation, at least not to the same extent, to contain inflation and guarantee industrial peace. Thirdly, transnational mobility has strengthened capital immeasurably against an immobile labour in a number of ways. Organized labour's co-operation is no longer necessary to achieve greater productivity or to introduce new methods of production. The freedom of the market place has given capital the power to secure compliance from workers, i.e. to achieve 'flexibility', with the implicit or explicit threat of moving out or investing elsewhere. Fourthly, membership in unions has declined – though the extent of decline varies – and in a number of countries such as the UK, the US and New Zealand draconian laws and practices have emasculated labour unions (King, 1987, pp. 118–20 on the UK; Moody, 1987, pp, 155, 160–62 on the US; Kelsey, 1995, Chapter 8 and OECD, 1996a, pp. 53–6 on New Zealand).

Finally, it must be recognized that with the collapse of state socialism as a rival social system to capitalism and the impracticality of Keynesian economic management in the globalized economy, there seems to be no viable alternative to neoliberal orthodoxy. The labour movement can help to get a social democratic government elected but the government may not be able to deliver much that is different from its conservative counterparts. Although modest measures, e.g. the minimum wage in the UK promised by Tony Blair's New Labour, remain possible, to a large extent labour is left to fight a rearguard action against unemployment and a weakening social safety net.

Traditionally, fighting unemployment and ensuring a reasonable programme of unemployment compensation have been major concerns of unions. It is clear that in both of these areas, labour has lost ground in most Anglo-Saxon countries. With parliamentary politics failing to make much of a difference, we are seeing more by way of protest demonstrations and industrial action, e.g. strikes, against job loss and cutbacks in social protection. Organized labour often provides the muscle for these protest movements. Continental Europe, where the labour movement is stronger than elsewhere, has witnessed such action in many countries (see pp. 68–9) – notably in Belgium, France, Italy and Germany. Among English-speaking countries Canada, for example, not normally associated with extra-parliamentary protest, has recently seen action against austerity policies on a scale unprecedented in the country. In the United States there are signs of a revival and revitalization of labour under new national leadership.

It is reasonable to conclude that despite its reduced power and effectiveness, organized labour as an established pressure group and as a protest movement is acting as a bulwark against the rapid deterioration of systems of social protection in many countries. Moreover, at a supranational level, European labour has helped to promote the Social Charter of the European Union (Silvia, 1991). In North America labour opposition to NAFTA resulted in a commitment on the part of each member country to fully enforce its existing labour legislation.

More generally, however, we see a major difference between countries of Continental Europe on the one hand and Anglo-Saxon countries on the other. Most of the former are still following an approach to societal management, including the economy and industrial relations, that is largely consensual and recognizes organized labour as a valued social partner. English-speaking countries on the other hand, with the US and New Zealand in the lead, are increasingly market-oriented and are seeking to achieve greater competitiveness and flexibility through deregulation and the weakening of social protection.

The Feminist Movement

The movement for fighting the unequal position of women in society is far from monolithic ideologically. For example it includes liberal, socialist and radical feminists[5] who hold very different views about state welfare (Williams, 1989; George and Wilding, 1994, Chapter 6; O'Connor, J., 1996, Chapter 1). Overall, however, it is fair to say that feminism has had an ambivalent relationship with the welfare state (Sainsbury, 1996; O'Connor, J., 1996, Chapter 1). While recognizing its potential for meeting women's needs, feminists have on the whole been highly critical of the welfare state for its patriarchal nature and its bureaucratic and undemocratic administration (Wilson, 1977; Williams, 1989; pp. 209–10; Harding, 1998). By and large the welfare state has been seen as reinforcing the subordination of women through its social policies and programmes (Sassoon, 1987; George and Wilding, 1994, pp. 143–9; O'Connor, K., 1996). Not surprisingly therefore, feminists have focused their attention on the 'gendering' of social problems and policies and exposing the myth of the gender-neutral universal welfare state (Sainsbury, 1994).

Sections of the feminist movement, especially those of a liberal or social democratic persuasion, have been more supportive of the welfare state, seeing in it the potential for developing policies that are equitable and beneficial for women (Ruggie, 1984; Sainsbury, 1996; O'Connor, J., 1996, Chapter 1). Socialist, radical and anarchist feminists on the other hand have tended to reject the welfare state as essentially capitalist and patriarchal and have looked towards developing alternative, democratically controlled services outside the state (Dominelli, 1991, pp. 266–70). In practice these divisions are not so rigid and there is some overlap as well as fluidity across these positions.

Feminist influence on social policy has taken a number of different forms. First, as a pressure group and as a social movement, feminists have advocated for specific services and legislation, e.g. in the areas of child care provision, affirmative action and violence against women (see McBride Stetson, 1990 on the US and Larkin and O'Neill, 1998 on Canada). Second, as voters, feminists have supported political parties or candidates who favour 'woman-friendly' policies (O'Connor, J., 1996). Third, feminist organizations have protested the retrenchment of social programmes and benefits which affect women adversely (Larkin and O'Neill, 1998).

Although feminists have been active at all three levels, the movement's organization and practice has differed across countries (Katzenstein and Mueller, 1987; Gelb, 1989). Globalization and austerity policies are impacting on all these forms of action (see for example, Brodie, 1995; Evans and Wekerle, 1997). The expansion of programmes and services which help women, e.g. day care, which is of major importance in view of women's rising labour force participation, are no longer on the political agenda. With the increasing trend towards deregulation of the labour market and government downsizing, affirmative action, pay equity and other such policies are being marginalized and eroded (Brodie, 1995; Yeatman, 1992; Kamerman, 1996; Yalnizyan, 1998). It should be noted, however, that the non-economic aspects of feminist demands, e.g. concerning reproductive rights and sexual orientation, are not directly affected by globalization although they come up against the patriarchal value orientation of neoliberalism. Meanwhile policies of cutbacks and privatization are transferring the burden of care – whether of young children, the frail, the sick or the disabled – from the public to the private sphere, which inevitably means an additional burden for women in families (Hooyman and Gonyea, 1995).

In sum, with financial retrenchment and government withdrawal from so-cial welfare services, the conditions in which feminist groups could advocate effectively for better services for women have changed fundamentally. The prospect of defending – not to say extending – social programmes which assist women is not very bright. True, as voters, women have exercised some leverage on political parties and governments and at least in North America, there is a clear gender gap. More women vote for candidates who support social programmes and government activism. Thus such measures as (un-paid) family leave, support for health insurance for Americans and the promise of spending more on education by the Clinton administration helped to swing 55 per cent of women voters over to Clinton compared with 37 per cent for Republican candidate Dole in the 1996 presidential election. This is impres-sive when we consider that men's votes were split evenly at 44 per cent for each candidate (*The Economist*, 1996a, p. 28).

It is not unreasonable, then, to suggest that to the extent that there is a gender gap, women's votes are having some influence in sustaining or even promoting social measures favoured by women. Even so, we should note the tightrope being walked by centrist administrations such as President Clinton's. Thus family leave, a popular measure passed by the first Clinton administration, is unpaid and exempts businesses with fewer than 50 employees (Baker, 1997).

The feminist movement *has* been active on its own and in coalition with labour and other groups in opposing government cutbacks and defending social programmes, and in advocating for disadvantaged groups (Kamerman, 1996; Evans and Wekerle, 1997). The effectiveness of these general protest movements is difficult to gauge. However, feminist writers have drawn atten-tion to 'women's relative powerlessness' compared to other interest groups in 'seeking to influence social policy' (Dominelli, 1991, p. 265). The reasons for this are many, including the 'structurelessness' and' 'organizational weak-ness' of the feminist movement.

In rejecting hierarchy and bureaucracy, the movement has functioned as a loose association of groups and activists, i.e. more as a 'new social move-ment' than as an organized pressure group, although in some countries, e.g. the US and Canada, the latter aspect has also been important (Gelb, 1990,

pp. 137–8, 154). Moreover, as a predominantly white, middle-class movement it has not necessarily been concerned with issues of poverty, deprivation
and inequality affecting lower-class and black women (Ryan, 1992, pp. 125–
7). Affirmative action and equity policies have 'benefitted white middle-class
women to a much greater extent than poor women and women of color'
(ibid., p. 125). Overall, an assessment made in the early 1980s, namely, that
'the ideological impact of feminism has been much greater than any changes
in women's material position' (Weir and Wilson, 1984, p. 102) would seem to
have general validity.

In summary, then, the second wave of the feminist movement beginning in
the US in the late 1960s arrived at a time when the Keynesian welfare state
was well entrenched. As far as social welfare is concerned, the feminist
movement has been mainly critical of service provision, seeking to expose its
gender bias and reliance on women's unpaid care work (Baines et al., 1991;
Sainsbury, 1994). Following the rise of neoliberalism, the retrenchment of
social citizenship has received a new impetus in the 1990s from a globalizing
economy. However, given the weakness of the feminist movement organiza-
tionally and its ambivalence towards the patriarchal welfare state, it cannot be
considered a major force in the defence of existing provision.[6]

Indeed instead of the feminist movement coming to the defence of social
rights it appears that the retrenchment of the welfare state is weakening the
feminist movement. For although feminists 'exposed the false universalism
of the ... welfare state' (Williams, 1992, p. 206), it was precisely the language of universality and social citizenship that helped to bring women into
the policy debate. On the terrain of the nominally universalistic and citizen-
ship-oriented KWS, feminists could challenge the de facto particularism and
inequity of gender-biased social policy (Brodie, 1995).

But now that globalization and neoliberal orthodoxy are working together
to privatize care and to commodify labour markets and human services, the
dialogue of equality and social citizenship is becoming increasingly marginal. Policies of targeting and selectivity, in focusing on income rather than
gender or race, are displacing the discourse onto the economic realm (ibid.).
With growing inequality and polarization of incomes, the position of lower-
class women is worsening while upper- and middle-class women seem in a
much better position to obtain services from the market. Indeed an Australian
feminist (Yeatman, 1992, p. 456) wonders if these women 'still share gender
class conditions with the majority of women locked into ... local environ-
ments of restricted collective consumption and declining public infrastructure'.
Janine Brodie, a Canadian feminist, makes a similar point regarding the
'degendering' of issues. With reprivatization and the targeting of benefits, she
argues, income, class and other categories are moving to the fore (Brodie,
1995, pp. 47–9, 73–5).

Moreover, in some countries such as Canada the feminist movement has been heavily funded by the state. Since its inception in 1972 the main umbrella organization of Canadian feminism, the National Action Committee on the Status of Women (NAC), has been funded by the government and by the late 1980s, some 60 per cent of its annual budget came from the federal government. In recent years funding has been cut by half and many special women's programmes have been eliminated (Bashevkin, 1994, p. 280). These cost-cutting measures have weakened the movement, especially with regard to its ability to influence social policy. This situation may be unique to Canada but more generally, the fact remains that globalization pressures and the restructuring of welfare along neoliberal lines is eroding feminist influence on social policy.

The Aged

The ageing of the population in OECD countries and the development of costly social programmes for the elderly, notably retirement pensions, has raised the question whether older citizens now constitute a significant interest group with a vested interest in the welfare state. In OECD countries the aged (over 65s) now constitute between 10 and 20 per cent of the population and of course, a higher percentage of the electorate. Moreover, compared with younger age groups, a higher proportion of the aged vote. In France the retired (not all of whom are aged) apparently comprise one-third of all voters (Gifford, 1990, p. 231). It is well-known – and feared in some quarters – that the proportion of the aged population will rise through the early decades of the next century, thus adding to the strength of this group.

No wonder the aged are seen as constituting a formidable group which will defend and perpetuate its vested interests in the welfare state. Indeed evidence from the US indicates that senior citizens are well organized and have been very successful, for example, in defending social security pensions (Day, 1990). Extrapolating from the US, it is tempting to argue that in all advanced industrial democracies, the aged are becoming redoubtable champions of pensions and health care as well as other relevant benefits and services. Hence democracies will be hard put to reform, let alone undo, their systems of public pensions and health care which in any case also enjoy popular support. If this is true, then we are confronted once again with a version of the 'irreversibility' thesis (with a perverse twist), this time not in the context of advancing neoliberalism, but rather globalization.

How valid is this gerontocratic dominance thesis? Let us note, first of all, that the nature and scope of senior citizens' organization and the nature of their political activity varies a good deal across nations. The gerontocratic thesis is based largely on the situation in the US and its validity will be considered below. What seems clear, however, is that the US is somewhat exceptional in having a strong and active seniors' organization with a successful record of lobbying. The two major organizations in the US – the American Association for Retired Persons (AARP) and the National Council of Senior Citizens (NCSC) – appear to be extremely active and involved in advocacy and in influencing policy more generally. This is particularly the case since the early 1980s before which, these organizations seem to have played a minor part in the development of seniors' programmes such as Medicare (Day, 1990, pp. 93–5).

The strength of the seniors' lobby was demonstrated most visibly in 1981 when President Reagan had to withdraw proposals for drastic cuts in social security, i.e., retirement and disability benefits. Since then policy-makers have been inclined to see older people 'as a formidable political force in their own right' (Day, 1990, p. 33). The aged are regarded as the 'clear winner' in the aftermath of the 1980s cutbacks, a group that has 'escaped every attempt at retrenchment' (ibid.). Indeed such is the perception of the power of the seniors' lobby among politicians that Congress dare not offend the aged; any benefit cuts have to be carefully disguised. However, senior citizens' organizations in other countries do not compare with those in the US in their lobbying power and political effectiveness.

In Canada, for example, seniors' organizations are more local, i.e. provincial and regional, rather than national in scope. And although senior citizens have been active as advocates and defenders of relevant benefits and programmes, the seniors' lobby is far less effective than in the US (Gifford, 1990). Substantial changes have occurred in programmes of income security for the aged and in medical care over the last ten years. Yet it appears that the aged have not been able to offer effective resistance to cutbacks.

In the UK where pensioners account for a quarter of the electorate, far-reaching changes have occurred in respect of retirement pensions – including the raising of the pensionable age for women from 60 to 65 – and long-term care. Again there is scant evidence that seniors' groups have been engaged actively with these issues, although other groups have been active on their behalf (Ginn, 1996, p. 143).

Overall the impression one has from West European countries is that while senior citizens' organizations do exist and engage in some advocacy, there is little to compare with the effective lobbying and campaigning typical of the aged in the US (Gifford, 1990, pp. 220–28; Ginn, 1996, p. 129). This does not preclude political action – of a reactive kind – on the part of the aged. Thus in the Netherlands, recently, plans to cut back pensions resulted in 'newly formed pensioners' parties' taking seven out of 150 seats in the general election (Milner and Tran, 1995, p. 11).

American exceptionalism can be explained by a number of factors. First, it is no secret that the fragmented political system in the US, with the President and two Houses of Congress, encourages lobbying and also makes it highly effective. Secondly, the absence of a party government and party discipline works in the same way. A third possible reason is that unlike European countries, the US lacks a strong labour movement and a social democratic party which could champion social rights, including those for the aged. Could seniors in other countries emulate their peers in the US and emerge as a strong pressure group? Such a possibility cannot of course be ruled out but seems unlikely at the moment.

Although a higher percentage of older citizens vote, there is little evidence to suggest that the aged act as a voting bloc (Binstock, 1992; Ginn, 1996). Older adults are as diverse as their younger counterparts in respect of level and source of income, education, religious affiliation, ethnicity and the like and these influence voting patterns of seniors as much as those of others. Nor can it be argued that narrowly defined economic interests alone decide how the aged vote.

For example in the American presidential election of 1984, the same proportion of older men (over 60) voted for Reagan as men of all age groups while a *higher* proportion of older women voted for Reagan than women of all ages (Binstock, 1992, p. 602). In the presidential election of 1996, a slightly higher percentage of the aged voted for Clinton, but the gap was much wider at the other end with a far higher proportion of the young (18–29 years) voting for Clinton (*The Economist*, 1996a, p. 28). In 1992 nearly half of the aged in Britain voted Conservative, apparently for the only party that did *not* promise to raise pensions substantially (Ginn, 1996, p. 128).

In fact pensions and other programmes for the aged remain among the most popular of social programmes for a number of reasons. First, the aged are generally perceived as an eminently deserving group. Secondly, everyone expects to reach the 'golden' years and in that sense has a stake in programmes for the aged. Thirdly, the financial and personal independence of the aged remains a concern for younger family members. Not surprisingly, support of programmes for the aged is strong and is likely to remain so. Thus pensions, health care for the aged and other seniors' programmes are likely to remain among the least retrenchable of social programmes.

Nonetheless, there are signs that the situation may be changing. For example, in the US 'compassionate ageism' is apparently giving way to 'conflictual ageism' (Ginn, 1996, p. 127). The question of intergenerational equity has been raised specifically in terms of older Americans monopolizing public resources. Indeed it is perhaps significant that even Lester Thurow, a well-known liberal academic, joins in the gerontophobic hysteria claiming that the 'needs and demands of the elderly have shaken the social welfare state to its foundations, causing it for all practical purposes to go broke' (Thurow, 1996, p. 97). Thurow envisions an intergenerational conflict in the coming years on the scale of class conflict in the past. Quite recently, an organization known as Americans for Generational Equity (AGE) has been formed to campaign for taking public funds away from 'self-sufficient' seniors. Financed by banks, insurance companies and health care corporations, AGE aims at promoting private pensions in place of publicly funded ones (Ginn, 1996, p. 127).

Clearly, in the neoliberal ideological climate of North America, which favours privatization and tax reduction, a political backlash is being engineered against programmes for the aged. Senior citizens are beginning to lose their status as a specially deserving group. In recent years Canadian senior citizens have been called upon to do more to fight the deficit (a fight which has now been won!). A somewhat milder version of the 'greedy geezer' argument prevalent in the US is also being heard in Canada (McDonald, 1995, p. 448).

The idea that the Canada Pension Plan could 'go broke' has been touted in the media and proposals to move retirement provision further towards the private sector have been discussed widely. It appears that 'newer and less than compassionate stereotypes of older workers/retirees' are helping to create changes in policies and programmes 'that may be, at best, indifferent to most older persons and downright punitive to others' (ibid.). Greater selectivity in pensions coupled with privatization could pave the way for a 'two-tiered retirement system: one for the rich and one for the poor' (ibid., p. 451). As pension reform in English-speaking countries shows (see pp. 48–9, 66), universal retirement programmes are not as sacrosanct as they appear to be. Neoliberalism has found a new and powerful rationale in globalization for reducing social expenditure. In this climate of opinion, seniors' programmes are likely to become vulnerable to privatization, reduction of benefits and a shift towards selectivity.

The 'imperatives' of a global economy, i.e. debt and deficit reduction, government downsizing and keeping taxes low, could help governments to retrench universal programmes without having to pay a political price. And as the framework of universality crumbles, the idea of social citizenship could become increasingly *passé*. As in the case of women, the retreat from universality and the public sphere could shift identities and solidarities away from age and more towards class.

Protest Movements

Extra-parliamentary protest seems to be on the rise in Western countries. With monetarism and fiscal austerity becoming almost bipartisan, parliamentary and electoral channels are failing to provide clear alternatives in social policy. Those adversely affected or threatened by unemployment, cutbacks in social protection and other policy changes have no alternative but to protest in any way they can.

In December 1995, France witnessed one of the largest demonstrations and strikes by public sector unions against reductions in pension benefits and increases in contributions. This three-week-long action had widespread public sympathy and support (Bensaid, 1996). France, whose political culture may be seen as distinctive in being conducive to such action, has not been alone in this. Germany has seen some large demonstrations, e.g. in June 1996, against austerity measures proposed by the government in order to meet the Maastricht criteria of budget deficit (Traynor, 1996, p. 3). Similar protests have occurred in other European countries, notably Spain, Italy and Belgium (Heller, 1996). Canada, a law-abiding and constitutional country by any standard, has seen protests and demonstrations in several provinces against draconian cutbacks (*Canadian Dimension*, 1997, pp. 3, 8–12).

How effective these forms of action have been in slowing down, blocking or reversing austerity policies is not easy to assess. Naturally the situation varies from one jurisdiction to another. In France as well as in other countries of Continental Europe protest seems to have been effective in slowing down or halting temporarily the push towards austerity. On the other hand the long-term course in social policy in Europe remains one of deficit reduction and curtailment of social spending.

The election of a socialist government in France pledged to a traditional social democratic approach in policy – that of fighting unemployment, maintaining social protection, raising taxes if necessary – and working to change the monetarist policies of Maastricht, is a significant departure from the tendency towards political convergence on the Right typified by the New Labour orientation of Prime Minister Blair in the UK (on France see, for example, Webster and Steele, 1997, pp. 1, 12; on the UK see Thompson, 1996; Elliott, 1996, p. 19 and *Guardian Weekly*, 1998, p. 10). Whether a return to the traditional social democratic management of capitalism promised by the Jospin government is feasible in the 1990s and beyond is a question whose importance reaches much further than France. It remains to be seen whether the Jospin government might prove to be a catalyst in turning the situation around.

CONCLUSIONS

This chapter has been concerned with the question whether and to what extent democracy is able to counter the pressures of globalization and help preserve social programmes and expenditures. It appears that electoral politics and party competition are proving ineffective in this regard, with parties of the Left and Right following a broadly similar agenda of private sector job creation, deficit control and downsizing of the social welfare state.

Public opinion remains strongly in favour of government responsibility for managing the economy in order to create jobs and maintain social programmes and benefits. Polls also show public willingness to pay taxes – indeed to pay more – to maintain and improve heartland services such as health care or pensions. Tax fairness, however, may be an important point here, since the tax burden has grown lighter at the top and heavier at the middle and the bottom end of the scale. There is virtually no evidence of people's disappointment or disillusionment with the welfare state. This is significant in light of two decades of ideological assault by the New Right on the 'nanny state' and its constant barrage of propaganda proclaiming that government is the problem, not the solution. It is also significant in light of the repudiation of the welfare state as patriarchal, bureaucratic and unresponsive by the new social movements on the Left.

The vast majority of people of all ages, sexes and races do not want to see these institutions dismantled. Thus while state socialism has all but passed into history and there is little enthusiasm for public ownership of business and industry, the institutions of social welfare are proving to be extremely popular and difficult to dismantle.

In light of strong public support for mainstream social programmes, frontal assault is often a difficult proposition. Retrenchment, therefore, has to be piecemeal and requires various strategies of concealment and subterfuge (Pierson, 1994). These can be quite effective and far-reaching, as the example of Canada shows. More importantly, globalization has provided right-wing governments with a new weapon in the form of external constraints and exigencies as the rationale for austerity policies and retrenchment. It thus helps to insulate unpopular policies from democratic pressures and by the same token, bars centre or left parties from pursuing alternative policies. True, many European nations have inherited a large welfare state from the golden age and, for the moment, seem to be able to hold on to them. But can they hold out against global pressures? This is an important point. The significance of cross-national differences in response to globalization is an issue we take up in the next chapter.

In contrast with political parties, interest groups and social movements seem to be in a better position to oppose welfare state retrenchment. Organized labour, despite its reduced power and strength, is playing an important part not only as a pressure group opposed to retrenchment but increasingly, by orchestrating extra-parliamentary action in support of the welfare state. At the very least it is acting to slow down, halt or limit retrenchment. It is possible that protest may lead to some rethinking, especially in Western

Europe, of at least the pace, if not also the direction, of change in social policy. But overall one has the impression that this opposition may be no more than a rearguard action which could halt the agenda of retrenchment only temporarily.

Among other interests involved with social programmes, we have briefly reviewed gender- and age-related groups and movements. Given the negative to ambivalent attitude of the feminist movement towards the patriarchal welfare state and given its diffuse and structureless nature, it is not surprising that the feminist movement is not at the forefront of resistance to welfare retrenchment. On the other hand women as public sector workers organized in unions and as individual voters are supporting policies of maintaining state welfare.

Age-related groups do not seem to be very well organized or effective outside of the US. In the US they have proven staunch defenders of social security and medical care and more recently, have begun to forge coalitions with other groups concerned with protecting social welfare. However, even in the US seniors may have peaked as an influential interest group. Although the aged will be growing as a proportion of the voting population in the coming years, there is not much evidence to suggest that they will act as a 'cohesive bloc', divided as they are in terms of income, source of income and many other characteristics that influence voting patterns and attitudes.

Indeed a review of both women and the aged as interest groups suggests that recent developments such as the move away from universality, the privatization of services and growing inequality of incomes is likely to weaken policy-related pressure groups spawned by the universalism and social rights orientation of the KWS.

In sum, electoral politics and pressure groups are able to provide a degree of resistance to welfare state retrenchment. But this opposition is reactive rather than proactive. What is lacking is a clear alternative to the neoliberal management of the capitalist economy in conditions of globalization. Although a good deal is heard nowadays about the 'third way' – between traditional social democracy and neoliberalism – the ideas and policies of its practitioners, such as Bill Clinton or Tony Blair, amount to a gentler and kinder version of neoliberalism rather than a different approach to the economy and social protection.[7]

At any rate it appears that organized labour could play an important part in mounting strong opposition to the policies of welfare state rollback and privatization favoured by globalizing market forces. Since it is national governments that must implement policy changes in response to the demands and wishes of global (and domestic) capitalism, strong extra-parliamentary action at the national level can thwart the agenda of no-holds-barred globalization. As the example of France shows, such action could also lead to changes at the parliamentary and political level. Even so, in the absence of an alternative model or at least a viable alternative strategy of employment and social protection, opposition is unlikely to be effective in the long run.

While the economy is becoming more global and commodified, systems of social protection remain locked into separate national enclaves reflecting the conflicts, compromises and priorities of a bygone era. At best it seems a matter of holding on to the status quo. Yet it is also becoming clear that the problems posed by globalization stem from decisions being taken at a supranational level – whether by global markets or IGOs of various kinds – albeit with national consent or connivance, and any definitive solution to the problem must also be sought at that level. We address this issue in the final chapter.

Before that, however, we need to examine globalization in a comparative perspective in order not to overgeneralize from the experience of Anglo-Saxon countries. This is the task of the next chapter.

NOTES

1. Minimum wage was virtually the only measure which distinguished the Labour Party's approach to social policy from that of the Conservatives in Britain in the early 1990s (George and Miller, 1994). A recent review of social and economic policies in seven OECD countries found the differences between parties and governments to be so minimal as to require 'close looking and sometimes even a magnifier to pin down these differences' (Muller, 1994, p. 48). What counts as 'sufficiently distinguished' or 'minimal' is obviously subjective, a matter of value judgement. See pp. 102–3 for a definition of 'left-of-centre' policy.
2. For an example of such policy differences see Castles and Pierson (1996) which contrasts Labour Government policies (in Australia and New Zealand) with their Conservative counterparts and with the policies of the Thatcher Government in Britain. However, to their conclusion that 'politics still matters', we would like to add a caveat namely 'but it matters a good deal less now because of the constraints of a globalizing economy'.
3. The policy of 'stealth' or disguised retrenchment practised by the Conservative Government in Canada in the 1980s and the open retrenchment of social expenditure by the Liberal Government in the 1990s brings out this contrast very clearly (Barlow and Campbell, 1995). No doubt in conditions of electoral democracy, subterfuge and disingenuousness will continue to form an important ingredient in the policy of cutbacks and retrenchment.
4. All three countries have seen a substantial drop in union membership and in the proportion of workers covered by collective bargaining. As well, legislation and/or anti-union practices have weakened unions substantially. For example in the UK, union density fell from 50 per cent in 1980 to 34 per cent in 1994. Workers covered by collective bargaining dropped from 70 per cent in 1980 to 47 per cent in 1993. Growth of part-time and other non-standard forms of employment has reduced the scope of unionism further (see Hutton 1995a, pp. 91–2; King, 1987, pp. 118–20; OECD, 1997d, p. 71, Table 3.3).
5. No distinction will be made between the 'feminist' and 'women's' movement nor between the academic–intellectual wing of feminism and the socio-political aspects of the movement. We must let the context decide the sense in which the term 'feminist' is used.
6. This is only true of the 'feminist' movement as such. Women as individual participants or as members of professional organizations, trade unions and voluntary associations, such as

nurses, teachers, public employees, social workers, sole support parents, immigrants or simply as concerned citizens have been at the forefront of the struggle against service cutbacks and benefit reductions.

7. Centre-left governments and parties, which do not subscribe to the neoliberal approach, have been groping for an alternative to the older forms of state-centred, 'tax-and-spend' policies on the one hand and the free market dogma of neoliberals on the other. The result is pragmatism giving rise to a variety of 'third ways' rather than *a* or *the* 'third way'.

5. Globalization in comparative perspective: Sweden, Germany and Japan

In this chapter we return to the question of the relationship between globalization and the welfare state, but from a comparative perspective. As pointed out in Chapter 1, our examination of globalization and its implications for social standards and social protection centred largely on the experience of Anglo-Saxon countries. However, throughout these explorations we have also pointed out that the trends and tendencies observed in these countries in respect of the labour market, industrial relations, taxation and social protection are much less in evidence elsewhere, notably in countries of Continental Europe. We made scant reference to Japan and East Asia, in part because the Asian pattern of welfare differs so substantially from its Western counterpart. Yet it is important to examine the thesis of globalization in relation to as wide-ranging evidence as possible in order to understand better the nature of relationships involved.

In this chapter, therefore, we draw on material from three countries, Sweden, Germany and Japan, in order to explore the connection between globalization and social policy. Each of these countries may be said to represent, as it were, a distinct type of welfare state regime as well as a 'culture realm'. Sweden is the leading welfare state among Nordic countries whose system of social protection is social democratic and based on the social citizenship model. Germany is the leading welfare state based on the Bismarckian social insurance model (Esping-Andersen, 1990). Finally, Japan is the leading industrialized nation of East Asia with a pattern of welfare very different from any that exist in the West (Goodman and Peng, 1996; Pempel, 1989). Moreover these countries, especially Germany and Japan, also differ from Anglo-Saxon countries in some other ways relevant to globalization, namely, the nature of financial and capital markets, corporate culture and industrial relations (Albert, 1993, pp. 106–13; Hutton, 1995a, Chapter 10). How is the relationship between globalization and social policy playing out in these countries? How is it different from the relationships observed in Anglo-Saxon countries?

SWEDEN

For social democratic Sweden the first and the most obvious implication of the greater openness of economies has been the end of full employment. Until the late 1980s Swedish unemployment was below 2 per cent. The situation changed dramatically in the 1990s. From 1.8 per cent in 1990, unemployment rose to 9.5 per cent in 1993 (from 2.1 to 12.5 per cent if those on active labour market measures are included) (Stephens, 1996, p. 45). This was the result of a severe economic crisis in 1990 which blew the social democratic hope of maintaining full employment and improving social protection completely off course. An austerity package had to be brought in which included reductions in social benefits. Other crisis measures followed (Stephens, 1996, p. 45; Olsson and McMurphy, 1993, pp. 253–6). Unemployment rose rapidly, while GDP fell between 1991 and 1993 (OECD, 1998, p. 225). Meanwhile Social Democrats changed their stand on Europe and decided to join the EU.

Unemployment has remained high (over 8 per cent in early 1998) and it appears that Swedish Social Democrats have given up on restoring full employment. This 'paradigm shift', according to Swedish policy analysts Olsson and McMurphy (1993, p. 267), has occurred largely as a result of globalization pressures. First, as discussed earlier (p. 20), given trade and financial openness, reflation in one country is no longer a viable option. Secondly, the free movement of money and capital has meant greater integration of the Swedish economy in the global market place. Hence budget deficits and high rates of inflation are punished by domestic as well as foreign capital.

Sweden's policy of full employment and high social expenditure was based on a corporatist compromise and consensus among organized labour, the state and employers. It included a system of centralized wage bargaining which helped to contain inflation and maintain wage equity, while institutionalized co-operation between social partners over labour market measures ensured flexibility and higher productivity in conditions of full employment. This system of centralized wage bargaining and neocorporatist approach to problem-solving has been undermined, mainly because employers have abandoned the consensual approach. Financial deregulation, which began in the mid-1980s, empowered employers hugely and they began to push hard for decentralized wage bargaining and other forms of labour market 'flexibility'. By the early 1990s the employers' organization (SAF) had withdrawn from membership and participation in a host of joint employer–employee organizations (Stephens, 1996, pp. 49–50; Wilks, 1996). Meanwhile business has used the exit option both as an opportunity to invest abroad as well as a leverage to get its own way in respect of domestic policy (Wilks, 1996, pp. 102–8; Kurzer, 1991, p. 19).

Whereas Swedish labour depends on Swedish capital to create jobs, the options of the latter are much wider. Swedish industry also happens to be one of the most centralized as well as internationalized among Scandinavian countries (Stephens, 1996, pp. 40–42; Wilks, 1996, pp. 101–6). Liberated from national dependence and enhanced in power, Swedish capital has asserted itself quite strongly against the social democratic government. Thus in July 1994 'the largest Swedish insurance company, Skandia, sold its 1.8 billion Skr. worth of government bonds ... in protest to the government's economic policy and stated that it would not purchase any further bonds unless the government took genuine steps to cut the budget deficit' (Wilks, 1996, p. 107). When in 1994 the Social Democrats seemed poised to win the election, managing directors of four of Sweden's largest international companies threatened publicly that 'investments totaling 50 billion Skr. would be at risk if taxes were raised' (ibid.). Peter Wallenberg, the head of the family that controls a substantial part of Swedish industry, threatened that the family's companies would locate abroad unless sustained cuts were made in public expenditure (ibid.).

Wage Solidarity and other Labour Market Changes

One of the characteristics of the Swedish welfare state has been the attempt to narrow wage differentials among workers. This was done in part by negotiating wages centrally and in part by eliminating low-productivity, low-wage employment and retraining workers through extensive labour market policies. It appears that along with centralized wage bargaining, Sweden's celebrated 'wage solidarity' policy has been a casualty of the employers' offensive. Its solidaristic wage policy was getting in the way of the 'flexibility' demanded by business in conditions of international competitiveness. Thus the

> collapse of centralized bargaining and the consequent disabling of the ... [solidaristic wage policy] set in motion a reversal of the considerable wage compression that had been under way for more than twenty years. By 1990, the variance in wages already had increased to the level of the mid-1970s (Olsen, 1996, p. 5).

Because of the high level of wage equality achieved by Sweden at the close of the golden age, the trend towards wage inequality still leaves Sweden with a far more egalitarian wage distribution than most countries, especially when compared with Anglo-Saxon countries. Moreover, thus far there is little to suggest that low-wage service jobs along the lines of the US and the UK will emerge in the near future (Stephens, 1996, p. 58). Nor is there any evidence that 'non-standard' employment along the lines of Anglo-Saxon countries (except for part-time employment which was a part of the Swedish policy of expanding public sector jobs to facilitate employment of women) is emerging.

On the other hand the trend line is clear. It is towards continuing high unemployment and increasing differentiation of wages. And although union membership and organization remain strong, employers and businesses are keen to move Sweden further along the road to labour market 'flexibility' (read low wages and working conditions). The radical reform of the labour market and labour relations carried out in New Zealand is being held up by the employers' association as the 'way to change' (Olsen, 1996, p. 15). There is every indication that Sweden will be moving further away from its homogeneous labour market and egalitarian wage structure.

see p. 42?

Taxation and Income Distribution

Taxation in Sweden was both high and steeply progressive. By 1980 the top marginal rate was close to 85 per cent and almost three-quarters of full-time employees had a marginal tax rate in excess of 50 per cent (Olsen, 1996, pp. 6, 8). On the other hand effective corporate tax rates were low by international standards. Pressure to reduce these high rates of taxation on upper incomes became stronger from about the mid-1980s as capital controls were relaxed and then abolished, giving business and the political Right increasing voice with the enhanced exit option. A radical tax reform was initiated in 1988 and continued through the early 1990s. Top marginal tax rates were dramatically lowered – from 85 per cent to 50 per cent – and the income tax on dividends eliminated. The scope of indirect and regressive taxes such as the value added tax (VAT) was extended and their rates increased.

Other changes, e.g. a move towards contributory insurance (described below) have occurred, making the tax-contribution system less progressive (ibid., p. 8). The emphasis on reducing taxes further is putting a cap on any further welfare state expansion. In any case tax increases, if they occur, are likely to be for reducing budget deficits rather than for expanding social programmes (Fulcher, 1994, p. 209). What is clear, however, is that these changes in taxation are likely to make after-tax distribution of incomes more unequal.

Social Protection

Sweden has been and still remains one of the most comprehensive and generous welfare states in the world. Nonetheless the 1990s have seen some substantial cutbacks and Sweden is beginning to scale down its social programmes. Major changes include a reduction in the level of benefits such as sickness, unemployment and parental leave from 90 per cent to 80 per cent of income. These benefits, which are taxable are to be reduced further (Olsen, 1996, p. 16). Waiting days have been introduced for unemployment and sickness insurance. Employers have been made responsible for the first 14 days of sickness insurance payments in order to give them more control over 'abuse'. Charges for prescription drugs, dental care and for visits to physicians have been increased. Annual grants to municipalities which provide various public services have been cut. Housing norms have been deregulated, rent controls weakened – resulting in rent increases in large cities – and housing subsidies cut (Stephens, 1996, pp. 45–8; Olsen, 1996, pp. 8–9).

Significant reforms have also occurred in the area of pensions and unemployment insurance. The basic pension – universal and non-contributory – has been reduced in value and the contributory state pension (ATP) subjected to thorough overhaul. A longer period of contribution is required for the full pension and benefits are now more closely related to contributions. Employees – and not just employers as in the past – are also required to pay contributions which are expected to rise (Stephens, 1996, p. 46; Gould, 1996, p. 80).

These changes may be considered 'qualitative' in that they move the Swedish social protection system away from the citizenship and towards a social insurance model (Esping-Andersen, 1996a, p. 14). There is also a stronger emphasis on 'workfare'. Work and training requirements have been strengthened 'substantially' in the unemployment insurance scheme, which has changed from a voluntary programme run by trade unions to a compulsory scheme with employee contributions (Stephens, 1996, p. 45; Gould, 1996, p. 81). Services in kind have seen some decentralization and a modest measure of privatization.

One area where private, i.e. work-related, plans have expanded substantially is in the area of pensions (Olsson and McMurphy, 1993, p. 262). Indeed it appears that 'the more privileged strata are exiting from the welfare state, be it in terms of private ... pension plans or services' and the failure to regularly upgrade state programmes may result in an exodus of elites, undermining 'the solidity of the welfare state foundations' (Esping-Andersen, 1996a, p. 14). Yet apparently the fiscal capacity to carry out this upgrading 'does not exist' (ibid.).

Social assistance has played a marginal role in Swedish social security since the system aspired to a social citizenship model of entitlement for benefits, together with full employment, high labour market participation of women and wage equality. With growing unemployment and other changes, e.g. restricted entitlement and level of benefits, the population on social assistance has continued to rise. It is estimated that in 1980 only 4 per cent of the population was living on social assistance. By 1992 the figure had doubled (Gould, 1996, p. 81). With growing long-term unemployment, the figures may be expected to rise further. Meanwhile municipalities were found to be paying varying rates of assistance, some far below the recommended rate. A standard rate of benefit payment has been recommended which the local authorities are expected to honour (ibid.).

Summary and Conclusions

The end of full employment and the beginning of chronic high unemployment is undoubtedly the most obvious impact of globalization on the Swedish welfare state. Changes in the structure of taxation and the pressure to reduce taxes further are also in line with globalization pressures. Changes in the labour market and income distribution seem, however, marginal so far compared with developments in many Anglo-Saxon countries. The same could be said about the nature of social programmes and benefits, even if the reductions in benefits and other changes outlined above are not unimportant. Moreover, the structure of universality has been maintained with little by way of means-testing of basic benefits. On the other hand looking ahead, the judgement that 'future reforms are likely to continue to lead to cuts in benefits and services' does not appear unreasonable (Gould, 1996, p. 91). What is also clear is that these changes have a great deal to do with the openness and internationalization of the Swedish economy (Huber and Stephens, 1998).[1]

As we have seen, financial globalization has provided Swedish capital – far more internationalized and concentrated than that of other Scandinavian countries – with the opportunity to undermine the integrated welfare state built by social democracy and the labour movement. Full employment has gone, centralized collective bargaining is a thing of the past and social programmes and benefits are being scaled back. No doubt Swedish big business would like to see the welfare state rolled back substantially. That this has happened only to a limited extent is due to a number of factors, chiefly political in nature. The fragmentation of the political Right, continuing support for social programmes in the country and a large and well-organized union movement are some of these. Besides, a time factor is also involved.

Although the Swedish model has been unravelling for some time it was not until the early 1990s that, in face of serious financial difficulties stemming from globalization, the social democratic attempt to shore up full employment and the comprehensive welfare state was finally abandoned. It is therefore 'early days' to see a great deal of change. What is more important is that the underlying framework, namely tripartite or neocorporatist institutions and ideology based on consensual decision-making, which sustained full employment and the social citizenship version of the welfare state in Sweden has eroded seriously, due chiefly to the active disengagement of Swedish capital. The importance of the neocorporatist framework is not in doubt. As Esping-Andersen (1996a, p. 15) observes, 'In the final analysis, the viability of the Swedish model will depend a lot on whether

Sweden's ... celebrated consensus-building infrastructure is capable of over-coming its present fragmentation'.

What our study suggests is that globalization has seriously weakened, if not fatally undermined, the pre-conditions of such consensus-building. For the problem is not essentially conjunctural or nationally specific (although it has those dimensions as well), but *structural*. Indeed the decline, if not fall, of the Swedish model is readily comprehensible in terms of the transformation of the power relations between capital and labour in Sweden. By denationalizing the economy and providing capital with an 'exit' option, globalization has strengthened capital's hand immeasurably against labour. And despite the continuing strength of Swedish labour, at least in terms of membership and organization (Olsen, 1996, p. 15; Huber and Stephens, 1998, p. 389), it is the empowerment of capital that has, in the last analysis, under-mined the Swedish way.

One other point needs to be made about the Swedish welfare state. Ever since the disarray of Keynesianism and the rise of neoliberalism, an impor-tant debate has centred around the retrenchment of the welfare state. Basically two views have emerged: one which sees the welfare state as largely 'irre-versible' and the other (in which I would place myself) which sees the welfare state as eminently reversible. One version of the irreversibility argu-ment, especially applicable to Sweden, is that advanced welfare states have 'grown to limits' anyway and that the future scenario for them is that of stability and continuity of a mature welfare state.

This scenario of stability and 'maturity', if it had any credibility before, has much less so in an age of globalization. The dynamics of global finance and capital are unlikely to 'leave well enough alone' and are likely to sideline democracy. Demands for the tax burden to be lowered and opportunities for privatization and profit-making to be enhanced are a part of this dynamic. The developments of the 1990s show that the Swedish welfare state is not immune from these influences.

GERMANY

In common with most Western industrial countries (West) Germany enjoyed conditions of buoyant employment during the golden age. Indeed such was the demand for labour that the country had to resort to 'guest workers', i.e. temporary immigrants. In the 1970s the German unemployment rate aver-aged below 4 per cent, but began to rise in 1981. In light of the litany of complaints about labour market 'rigidity' causing high unemployment in Germany, it is worth noting that *West German* unemployment was lower than the US's until at least 1992, although reunification with East Germany in

1989 pushed the overall German rates higher (OECD, 1998, p. 246). Unemployment is now in double digits and is likely to remain high. Unlike the Swedish Social Democrats, West Germany's Christian Democrats (voted out of office in 1998 after 15 years) did not make any serious attempt to maintain full employment. Quite apart from the difficulties resulting from unification, Germany's strict monetarism and fear of inflation means that Keynesian-style reflation is unlikely to be attempted. Moreover, membership in the European Union and now in the EMU brings in its train further constraints on national policy-making.

Germany's labour market is highly regulated, especially in comparison with that of Anglo-Saxon countries (OECD, 1994e, pp. 92–5; Streeck, 1993, pp. 146–8). Those in employment are well paid and also enjoy reasonable job security through employment protection laws and institutionalized collective bargaining. As a corollary those outside find it difficult to get into the labour force, making for the typical 'insider/outsider' divide. However, the unemployed are – and thus far have been – reasonably, though not generously, compensated (Esping-Andersen, 1996b, pp. 70, 79–80). German employers, as well as minority right-wing parties and IGOs such as the OECD and IMF, are strongly in favour of reducing unemployment benefits, weakening employment protection and in other ways making the labour market more 'flexible' (OECD, 1997e, pp. 134–5; Greider, 1998, pp. 365–6).

Thus far changes along these lines in the system of unemployment benefits and employment protection have been minor (Neyer and Seeleib-Kaiser, 1995, p. 33; OECD, 1997e, pp. 122–5). But pressure is building for further changes. While the Anglo-Saxon solution to job creation still looks like an unlikely development in the near future, a secondary labour market in 'non-standard' jobs is apparently growing in the informal economy and could lead to the development of a dual labour market (Greider, 1998, p. 373; Norman, 1997, p. 1). At any rate, no alternative solutions are in sight for creating jobs and reducing unemployment or indeed for moving towards a system of basic or citizen's income. But labour market issues are connected with the broader social market economy of Germany and the system of social partnership.

Germany's 'social market' economy is based on a consensual approach to industrial relations, namely social partnership between employers and unions. Collective bargaining is centralized and industry-wide. The system of 'co-determination' which embodies the principle of partnership, gives workers a significant presence on the supervisory boards and works councils of firms. Labour laws lay down rules of employment protection. Besides, the principle of making decisions on the basis of consensus makes it difficult for firms to dismiss workers (Albert, 1993, pp. 110–13; Bowley and Studemann, 1997, p. iv). Hence 'inflexibility' of the labour market has become a matter of public concern and debate in Germany of late. As might be expected, employers – both large and small – want greater 'flexibility' in matters of wage determination, hiring and firing as well as labour practices. Whether as a rationalization for wresting control away from workers or in response to greater competitiveness and other pressures stemming from globalization, employers are showing a great deal of concern over these issues (*The Economist*, 1996b, p. 19). Some openly express a preference for the American 'solution', i.e. less union interference, a weaker social safety net, fewer worker benefits and lower wages (Greider, 1998, pp. 365–8; Bowley and Studemann, 1997, p. iv).

The observation that 'since the spring of 1996 the whole German system of partnership between capital and labour has been falling apart' (Martin and Schumann, 1997, p. 130) may be an exaggeration, but indicates current trends. Increasingly companies are finding ways of getting around existing wage agreements or are simply pulling out of employers' associations. The threat of moving existing operations abroad and investing outside Germany is being used to gain concessions from workers (ibid.; Bowley and Studemann, 1997, p. iv).

It appears that Germany's celebrated consensus culture is weakening – at least in the area of labour relations – and the 'American' approach is gaining ground. One of the main reasons for this is that firms and their top executives are under pressure from the transnational money market, 'the real power centre of globalization' while cross-border trade in stocks and shares is proving a 'powerful solvent of national ties' (Martin and Schumann, 1997, p. 129). With foreign investors such as pension funds and mutual funds buying up shares in German companies, pressure for profits and performance is growing. The German capital market differs in important ways from that of Anglo-Saxon countries and corporations have been oriented to 'stakeholders' rather than 'stockholders' (Albert, 1993, pp. 106–13; Woolcock, 1996, p. 183). This is being reversed and the process is likely to go further. The consequences for the German social partnership approach could be far-reaching (Martin and Schumann, 1997, pp. 129–30).

Income Distribution and Taxation

Although changes in income distribution and taxation in Germany are modest in scale, they are nonetheless in the same direction as in Anglo-Saxon countries. Wage and salary differentials are still narrow but the distribution of income and wealth is becoming more disparate. As Vinocur (1997, p. A20) explains, 'The essence of the new disparity in incomes is that revenue from capital is accumulating much faster than that from wages'. Thus earnings from salaries rose only 10 per cent since 1991 but returns from capital rose by 40 per cent. At the same time revenue from non-wage income dropped sharply in the 1990s, suggesting enhanced opportunities for tax avoidance and for minimizing taxes on capital income (ibid.). Until recently, the pattern and rates of taxation had changed little in Germany. For example, between 1976 and 1992 the top income tax rate of the central government fell by only 3 per cent compared with 43 per cent in the UK and 39 per cent in the US (Sandford, 1993, p. 12, Table 2.1).

Recent reform proposals, however, seek to reduce the top rate of income tax substantially – from 53 per cent to 39 per cent. Corporate tax rates as well as withholding taxes on dividend payments are also to be cut (OECD, 1997e, p. 129). According to OECD (ibid.) the rationale for these changes is that proposed corporate tax rates 'will be closer to world levels and foreign investors would be placed on an equal footing'. An example of how cross-border investment and international tax competition are holding down tax rates is provided by Germany's attempt to levy a withholding tax on interest. It resulted in a 'massive outflow of funds to Luxembourg' which did not have such a tax (Owens, 1993, p. 31).

Social Protection

Unlike the Swedish welfare state with its social citizenship orientation, the German welfare state is based firmly on the social insurance model. Employers and employees each contribute 20 per cent of wages to finance social security with pensions, medical care, sickness and unemployment benefits as the major programmes. A variety of social insurance funds, partly differentiated by occupational status, make the German welfare state into a status-maintaining system, helping to reinforce rather than mitigate market differentials. This strong labour attachment model was attuned to the era of full employment (male). Now with large-scale and persistent unemployment as well as the growth of non-standard forms of employment, it is becoming less satisfactory as a basis for social security, since a growing part of the population (including the young) can no longer be entitled to benefits or to an adequate level of benefits such as pensions (Clasen and Gould, 1995, pp. 191–2).

On the other hand the legitimacy of and general support for the contributory insurance approach is quite clear. Thus a new compulsory long-term care scheme for the infirm and elderly, introduced in 1995, is based on social insurance. In part this measure was a response to the rising cost of social assistance for the care of the aged shouldered by municipalities and other lower-level governments (ibid., p. 193). Unlike Anglo-Saxon nations, Germany, along with many other European countries, has made only marginal reductions in its social programmes thus far. Besides, it has added the new long-term care programme to its range of social benefits.

However, globalization pressures have triggered a debate in Germany about loss of competitiveness due to generous social benefits, large social expenditure and high non-wage labour costs (Clasen and Gould, 1995, p. 192). Thus 'immediately after the reelection of the Conservative–Liberal coalition in October 1994, employers' organizations started a campaign in favour of a wholesale reconstruction, including retrenchments, of social policy provision' (ibid.). These demands have found positive echoes within the ranks of Free Democrats as well as among important sections of the Christian Democratic Party. More recently, in order to meet the Maastricht convergence criteria Germany has been under pressure to reduce the budget deficit by shrinking the social state. Chancellor Kohl put together a substantial package of benefit reductions amounting to about 2 per cent of GDP in 1997 alone (*The Economist*, 1996b, p. 18).

Faced with strong protests, the government rescinded some of the proposed reductions, e.g. in unemployment benefits, but went ahead with the others. Sick pay has been cut from 100 per cent to 80 per cent of the basic wage. State pensions are to be reduced from 70 per cent of the net average wage to 64 per cent albeit over a 30-year period. The early retirement age for women is to rise from 60 to 65 and for the long-term insured, from 63 to 65. Entitlement to unemployment insurance benefits and unemployment-related income support has been restricted. Early retirement provisions for the unemployed have been tightened (OECD, 1997e, pp. 121–5; *The Economist*, 1996b, p. 18). Germany, along with ten other European nations has qualified for the European monetary union by bringing its deficit to within 3 per cent of GDP (see p. 40). However from now on, apart from globalization pressures, Maastricht criteria are also likely to keep a lid on social spending.

Summary and Conclusion

Thus far the German social market economy and the welfare state remain far more intact than the Swedish social economy and welfare state. No doubt the system of financing – based on insurance contributions rather than direct taxation – as well as the system of benefits – which reflects the market and status situation of the work-force – has something to do with the acceptance of the system by economic elites and the political Right. The continuing strength of the German economy is yet another source of support. Hence there remains a good deal of consensus among employers and employees about retaining the system and managing with piecemeal rather than systemic reforms. The social market economy, with the social insurance model of social security as a key component, is well entrenched and barring a shock to the system or crisis of some kind, changes are likely to be small scale and gradual.

On the other hand as we have seen, pressures are building up on the grounds of global competition for more radical, systemic changes along Anglo-Saxon lines. The catalyst for change could be the threat of investing abroad. In 1995 German industry outward investment exceeded inward foreign investment by 37 billion DM. For German business Central European countries where wages are 'around a tenth of domestic levels', are proving particularly attractive (*The Economist*, 1996b, p. 18). Thus even as unemployment grows and manufacturing employment declines in Germany, business is investing, and threatening to invest, abroad. No wonder that business demand for greater 'flexibility' is beginning to make an impact (ibid.).

In any case the view of the German economy as 'inflexible' and 'burdened' by protective labour relations and high labour costs (both wage-related and non-wage) is being promoted vigorously by the Bundesbank and the German Employers' Organization (Glasman, 1997, p. 135). Meanwhile capital exit and financial globalization are acting as major influences towards compromising the social market economy and shrinking the social safety net. Albert's remarks (1993, p. 190) have a prophetic ring about them: 'financial globalization is the principal means by which the ultraliberal model is disseminated throughout the world. Its power is such that even the best-organized economies – the Rhine economies – are unable to fight back effectively.'

JAPAN

The Japanese pattern of social protection differs significantly from that of Western industrial countries (Pempel, 1989; Gould, 1993; Goodman and Peng, 1996). It is distinguished by a policy of full employment, sustained through a commitment to 'lifetime employment' by firms and employees and a dual labour market in which a substantial part of the labour force is employed in small firms at low wages and with limited benefits. The other main feature of the Japanese welfare system, related to the first, is its heavy reliance on employer-provided or work-related benefits, notably pensions and housing but also medical care, supplementary family allowances and family leave. Not surprisingly, the scope of state welfare programmes and the level of social expenditure as well as taxation in Japan have remained low, for example, well below the OECD average.[2]

Spectacular economic growth after the Second World War coupled with the desire to 'modernize', i.e. to catch up with the West in welfare provision, led to a rapid growth of state welfare in Japan. Japanese social expenditure grew at the fastest rate among OECD countries during the period 1960–75 and doubled as a percentage of GDP between 1960 and 1981 (OECD, 1985,

p. 21, Table 1). Basic state programmes such as pensions, medical care, unemployment benefits and family allowances were in place by the early 1970s. However, following the oil price shock of 1973, enthusiasm for developing a system of comprehensive state welfare paralleling the West cooled considerably (Goodman and Peng, 1996, pp. 203–4).

By the early 1980s the emphasis had shifted back to the Japanese way of welfare, i.e. reliance on extended family support and work-related benefits. As Goodman and Peng (ibid., p. 204) remark: 'The idea of developing a Western-style welfare state was actually only around a fairly short period of time and perhaps never took root'. Thus despite some advances in state provision, Japanese welfare remained centred in the workplace with the rather special employer–employee relationship characteristic of Japan. The reforms of 1981 implemented a series of cutbacks and restrictions. The pensionable age was to rise from 60 to 65, albeit over a period of 20 years. Contribution rates for pensions and health insurance were increased. Free medical care for the elderly, begun in 1973, was finally ended in 1982 (Goodman and Peng, 1996, p. 204; Lee, 1987, p. 251). The rapid ageing of the population in Japan has been made a matter of great national concern from the viewpoint of the rising cost of financial and health care and has tended to dominate thinking about social protection in the 1980s and 1990s.

Japan's economy performed very well during the 1980s, with higher economic growth, lower unemployment and lower budget deficits than other G7 countries (OECD, 1995c). Japan seemed to have been vindicated in its rejection of the Western model of the 'tax and spend' welfare state and in its reliance on its own way of running the economy and providing welfare (Gould, 1993; Maruo, 1986, pp. 76–7). No wonder Japan was seen as showing the way not only in respect of methods of production and management practices, but for some observers also in respect of social welfare, i.e. in limiting the scope of the state and assigning a larger role to other welfare providers (Gould, 1993).

The experience of the 1990s has, however, turned out to be very different. Whereas most Western countries recovered within a couple of years from the recession of 1990, Japan has been mired in stagnation and recession throughout the decade. Repeated economic stimuli in the form of substantial state spending on infrastructure have failed to set the economy on the growth path. Indeed at the moment (early 1998) Japan's economy is officially in recession. Meanwhile unemployment has climbed to more than 4 per cent and the budget deficit has increased substantially. Ironically it is Japan, a non-Western country, that has tried the Keynesian medicine of reflation in a big way. Unfortunately it has had a somewhat limited impact because of reasons other than those that have made it virtually unworkable in smaller economies (Chorney, 1996, pp. 371–2; Gee, 1998, p. D4).

To understand Japan's problems better we need to look briefly at the nature of the Japanese economy. It is a two-tier economy in that it combines a highly efficient export-oriented sector represented by Toyota, Sony, Hitachi and other big names with a large and substantially less efficient domestic sector of services and small producers. Moreover the Japanese domestic economy is highly regulated – both formally and informally – justifying the label of a 'closed' economy (Thurow, 1996, pp. 200–203; Greider, 1998, p. 375).

Undoubtedly many features associated with globalization do not apply to Japan. Thus 'free' trade has made rather limited headway in Japan since non-tariff barriers have effectively restricted foreign competition. As a result, Japanese consumers pay a good deal more for many products (Thurow, 1996, p. 202). Again market forces do not work in the Japanese capital market in the same way as they do in Anglo-Saxon countries. There is a good deal of cross-shareholding between banks and industrial firms and among industrial firms themselves (Kester, 1996, pp. 115, 127–9). The 'cosy' relationship that prevails as a result has permitted banks to lend money freely to companies (in which they may hold shares) resulting in huge bad loans in the 1990s (Gee, 1998, p. D4; Brummer and Watts, 1998, p. 19). Japan's financial liberalization, i.e. the removal of capital controls, is fairly recent and the inflow of capital is still rather limited.

The upshot is that despite its vast export trade, substantial investment abroad, and the internationalization of large enterprises, Japan Inc. remains very much a protected economy. It is this relative insulation from the sway of market forces that has enabled Japan to maintain its enterprise-centred system of full employment and welfare benefits. The less efficient but labour-intensive domestic sector of the economy helps maintain employment as does the 'lifetime employment' system of large and medium-size firms.

The broader social norm that Japanese employees will not be dismissed by the company as long and as far as possible means that 'millions of redundant people' remain on the company payroll even in times when profits are falling (Greider, 1998, p. 375). This makes sense in so far as Japan's welfare system is embedded in the enterprise itself. Private sector jobs for all – or at least all adult males – together with company-provided benefits, has been and remains the essence of the Japanese system of welfare. It is this that is now threatened by encroaching globalization.

Enter Globalization

Japanese firms have been setting up manufacturing plants overseas for quite some time now. In part the objective is to capture market share, e.g. by locating in Europe or North America, and in part it is to take advantage of lower labour and other costs, e.g. when locating in East Asia or Latin America

(Castells, 1998, pp. 231–2). Because of the commitment to maintain full employment at home, this has had only a marginal effect on the Japanese labour market. Unlike Germany, therefore, we do not see, thus far, Japanese employers using the threat of capital exit to scale down social protection or wages.

As we have seen, social spending as well as taxes are quite low in Japan. Furthermore if the labour market is 'rigid' in terms of employment security, it is quite 'flexible' in terms of wages, working conditions and workplace practices. Unemployment benefits are low with limited duration and strict conditions of eligibility (OECD, 1995c, pp. 127–9). Social cohesion, economic nationalism as well as company unionism make for worker compliance and wage moderation. Moreover income distribution in Japan has been and remains far more egalitarian than in most Western countries and compares favourably with that of Scandinavian countries. True, inequality has increased somewhat in recent years, but the change so far has been slight (Pempel, 1989, pp. 155, 180; Sullivan, 1997, p. 17).

Meanwhile as capital mobility, freer trade and financial deregulation have gathered momentum world-wide and as market forces have become more ascendant, Japan has come under greater pressure to open up its domestic economy to international competition. More recently, the long period of stagnation and recession has exposed the weaknesses of Japan's financial system, notably the banking sector, which relies a good deal on the norms of trust and 'accommodation' rather than on impersonal market-oriented criteria of performance and other objective standards in its dealings. Thus Japan, which only a decade ago was riding high in terms of economic growth and seemed to be setting the standards for competitiveness, is now flat on its back as it faces what might be the most serious problem of the post-WW2 era, namely, the reforms and adaptations necessary for the successful transition to a post-Fordist, post-industrial globalizing economy (Motohashi and Nezu, 1997; Gee, 1988, p. D4).

A radical deregulation and transformation of Japan's domestic economy could result in mass unemployment as companies restructure to meet foreign competition and let go of redundant labour, numbering in the millions. It could spell the end of the company-based workplace system of welfare (Greider, 1998, pp. 375–9; Castells, 1998, pp. 232, 241). If full employment and company welfare were to go under, the Japanese system of welfare as we have known it since WW2 would come to an end.

What would replace it? A Japanese-style residual form of welfare with high unemployment, low state benefits and reliance on the market, the extended family and charities? Or would Japan be able to fix its economic problems with piecemeal reforms, leaving the main elements of its system more or less intact? These are the imponderables as Japanese society feels the impact of the changing global market economy and the inevitable slowing down of growth in its now mature post-industrial economy. Meanwhile Japanese society is rapidly ageing and the rising cost of pensions, health and social care for an ageing population has emerged as a matter of serious concern (Goodman and Peng, 1996, pp. 204).

Summary and Conclusion

The Japanese welfare system forms an integral part of the relatively protected and closed Japanese domestic economy. Full employment based in the private sector and social security benefits provided by the employer constitute the essence of what is distinctive about the Japanese welfare system, although it has substantial state underpinning by way of basic social programmes. Until the late 1980s, the Japanese way of welfare looked fairly secure and compared with Western countries, Japan seemed well positioned in terms of labour market flexibility, low taxation and low state spending to remain economically competitive and dynamic.

This picture has changed in the 1990s. Japan's economy has been mired in sluggish growth and recessions. There are serious problems in the banking and financial sector. Pressures stemming from globalization and other changes, including the maturity of Japan's economy itself, have at the very least put the Japanese socio-economic system on the defensive. Reforms are apparently needed to revitalize the Japanese economy and to put it on the road to sustained growth. Some Japanese businesses and others are calling for deregulation, reduction in state welfare and lower taxes. Reforms, depending on their nature and extent, could have serious implications for the Japanese system of social protection, i.e. full employment and job security as well as company welfare. In some ways Japan faces the dilemma that the Swedish welfare state had to face earlier. Can full employment be saved in a globalized economy? Or will the mounting cost in terms of loss of dynamism, competitiveness and low profits push towards a market-based solution?

However, Japan's problem is virtually the reverse of Sweden's. Whereas Sweden has been under pressure to reduce its high level of social spending and taxation and scale down state welfare, Japan could be faced with a substantial *increase* in the scope of state welfare. Once full employment and job security disappear, corporate welfare, the lynchpin of the Japanese system, will be weakened seriously. Will the state take up the slack and move towards a European-style welfare state or will it go the American way of residual welfare? Or will Japan come up with its own home-grown version of 'creative conservatism' in this regard?

DISCUSSION

Do these three countries show similar trends in connection with globalization to those we have observed earlier in Anglo-Saxon countries? We shall look at full employment, the labour market, taxation and social protection in turn and then draw some general conclusions.

Two of the three countries examined, i.e. Sweden and Germany, have abandoned full employment. In the case of Sweden we see very clearly the overwhelming odds created by financial deregulation in general and by capital mobility in particular against full employment. After some two decades of heroic effort to save full employment, Swedish Social Democrats had to concede defeat. On the other hand, Japan is still holding on to its full employment policy based on private sector jobs and lifetime tenure. But for how long? As we have seen, it is largely by insulating its domestic economy from foreign competition that Japan has been able to sustain full employment. Pressures are building up for greater openness and deregulation of the economy in order to allow more competition. This does not bode well for the future of Japanese full employment. As the domestic economy becomes more integrated into the world economy, it is unlikely that full employment can be sustained.

Labour market organization and wage inequality in these countries show a rather different picture. The transformation of the labour market that has taken place in Anglo-Saxon countries with increasing polarization between good and bad jobs, growing inequality of wages and incomes, job insecurity, and growth of non-standard employment has no counterpart in these countries. Or at least not yet. Nonetheless, the trend line is broadly in the same direction. In both Sweden and Germany pressure for change is towards greater wage differentiation, lower wages, less job security and more decentralized wage bargaining. Demand for greater labour market flexibility and more free play of market forces is pushing broadly in the direction of developments in Anglo-Saxon countries. Japan is again different in that although the labour market is 'rigid' in terms of job security and tenure, it is highly 'flexible' in terms of employee compensation, wage dispersion, workplace practices and decentralized bargaining. Thus Japan appears to have its own version of 'flexibility' as a part of its system of full employment, job security and company welfare.

Changes in the system of taxation in Sweden and more recently in Germany are broadly in the same direction as in Anglo-Saxon countries. These include a reduction in the top rates of income taxes and easing of corporate and capital taxes. These changes, coupled with a shift towards consumption taxes and insurance contributions, e.g. in Sweden, are making for greater tax regressivity. The rationale for these changes flows from globalization, i.e. to make the tax system more investor-friendly and to provide incentives for wealth creation in conditions of capital mobility and tax competitiveness among nations. Once again, Japan presents a different picture. The overall incidence of taxation is much lower in Japan, but within the context of a progressive framework of pre-tax income and wealth distribution as well as taxation. Although the top personal rate of taxation (central government) has come down from 75 per cent in 1980 to 50 per cent in 1990, it remains higher than OECD and EU averages and, at 50 per cent, corporate tax rates are also high. Moreover, the top personal rate of taxation (combined central and local rate) is higher than that of Sweden (Owens, 1993, pp. 30–35, Tables 1, 3 and 4). Although some voices are being raised in favour of reducing top rates further, they are still rather muted (Sullivan, 1997, p. 17).

Of the three countries, Sweden has changed the most in the area of social protection. Social security benefits have been reduced, albeit from what was a very high level of social provision. From a largely citizenship-based approach the system of social security has moved towards a social insurance-type provision with benefits linked to contributions. However, the overall structure of universality is being maintained and thus far there is little to suggest that reforms along neoliberal lines are likely. Nonetheless pressure to reduce state benefits further and to allow more scope for non-state forms of welfare provision is likely to continue. Unlike Sweden, Germany's insurance-based system of social protection has seen only marginal changes, mainly some trimming of benefits. It appears that short of an economic crisis or other shocks to the system, only piecemeal changes are likely in the near future.

Japan is once again different in that its level of social expenditure has been and remains far below the OECD average. The decision to rein in development towards more comprehensive state welfare in the 1980s and the cutbacks legislated in 1981 ensured that the role of the state would remain one of providing a basic floor of social programmes supplemented by company welfare and extended family support. More recently, the ageing of the population and the resulting cost implications for social welfare have emerged as major concerns and the basic pensionable age has been raised from 60 (which is quite low in view of a much longer life expectation) to 65. On the other hand a home care insurance programme for the aged has been put in place (see Chapter 6, note 2).

Interestingly, Japan offers an example of 'social protection by other means' in which corporate welfare, i.e. a job for life together with social benefits, has been a key element. Economic developments associated with globalization are threatening to undermine this particular form of social protection. Japan could therefore face a problem opposite to that facing advanced welfare states in the West. If unemployment grows and corporate welfare is reduced substantially, Japan may be faced with the prospect of extending rather than retrenching the scope of state welfare.

Two other countries that have historically developed 'social protection by other means' – based on a protectionist economy, controlled immigration, full employment and wage regulation – are Australia and New Zealand. In recent years both countries have dismantled a good part of the old system (although in somewhat different ways) which could only function within an economy insulated from outside pressures. Although Japan is culturally quite distinct and has a much larger economy, in essence it faces a similar problem of adaptation. No system of social protection seems immune from the pressures stemming from the openness and greater internationalization of economies.

Although the relationship of each of the three countries to globalization is unique, there are also some commonalties. First, to a greater or lesser extent, all three countries show that globalization – openness of economies, freer trade and greater scope for market forces – presents a challenge to *national* strategies of economic growth and social protection developed during the more autarchic period of welfare capitalism. Second, in each country the system of social protection forms a part of a wider framework of socio-economic institutions and corresponding values and attitudes. The kind of reforms demanded by globalization, i.e. to move the economy and society in a neoliberal direction, thus challenge the system as a whole, based as it is on values and institutions other than those of neoliberalism. Since substantive change in one part of the system involves corresponding changes in the others, the integration of the system is threatened. Globalization pressures therefore meet with considerable resistance and support for the status quo, that is adaptation with minor reform, remains strong.

Third, it appears that in all three countries the welfare system represents a legacy of the past rather than a pointer to the future. Overall, the existing pattern is being upheld as both feasible and desirable but the approach is pragmatic and tentative. What seems to be missing is a sense of confidence in the national system as a model for the future. By contrast the strength of the neoliberal model of social economy espoused by globalizers lies in its clear articulation of reforms which can be generalized across nations and which would seem to be in tune with the globalizing economy.

In sum, countries as far removed from the Anglo-Saxon family of nations as Sweden, Germany and Japan are feeling the impact of globalization and associated changes. Although responses differ – and are not the same as those we have seen in Anglo-Saxon countries – the pressure for change is broadly in the same direction as that occurring in Anglo-Saxon countries. Globalization – in the form of greater financial and trade openness – appears to be a strong levelling force which, in the long run, threatens to transform the discrete social economies of nation states.

NOTES

1. Garrett (1998, pp. 138–44) argues that Sweden's economic difficulties and high unemploy-ment were the result of policy errors, notably pegging the Krona to the D-mark, and had little to do with globalization. While policy errors may have made the situation worse it is somewhat unconvincing to suggest that nothing else was involved. Garrett's economic functionalism and positivistic approach to globalization misses out almost entirely on the class and power relationships involved in financial liberalization. Policy errors cannot explain the decline of Swedish corporatism which began in the 1980s nor can they explain the retreat from progressive taxation and the social citizenship approach to social welfare. For a very different view of why the Swedish model ran into problems see Weiss (1998) who also believes that endogenous rather than exogenous factors are to blame. Huber and Stephens (1998) provide a more balanced and nuanced interpretation of social democratic corporatism in the context of internationalization.

2. Japan's public expenditure on social protection was only 11.57 per cent of GDP in 1990 compared with an average of 21.61 per cent for OECD countries (calculated from OECD 1994d, p. 59, Table 1b) and tax revenue only 29.1 per cent of GDP in 1993 compared with the OECD average of 38.7 per cent (OECD, 1995d, p. 72, Table 1).

6. The logic of globalization revisited

In this chapter we revisit the 'logic of globalization' set out in the form of seven propositions or theses in Chapter 1. What does our exploration of trends and developments in Anglo-Saxon countries as well as the others reviewed in the preceding chapters tell us about these theses? Let us make it clear that we have not been involved in 'testing' these 'hypotheses' except in a loose discursive sense. Rather the idea of these propositions was to structure arguments and evidence around specific issues and relationships concerning social policy and globalization. We shall discuss each of the seven propositions briefly in light of the material presented in the preceding chapters.

Proposition 1

Globalization undermines the ability of national governments to pursue the objectives of full employment and economic growth through reflationary policies. 'Keynesianism in one country' ceases to be a viable option.

Of the seven propositions this is undoubtedly the one that seems to find the strongest support from the evidence we have considered. Financial and trade openness of economies has made it virtually impossible to use Keynesian strategies of reflation in order to maintain full employment and generate stable growth. Heroic efforts of countries like Sweden attest to this fact. Japan, whose economy differs in important respects from that of Western countries, has also tried Keynesian stimulation but with poor results. However, the reasons for the lack of success of reflationary policy in Japan are rather different.

During the Keynesian era the expansion of the welfare state also meant a large growth of public sector jobs. Some social democratic regimes, e.g. those in Scandinavia, used this as a deliberate strategy of creating jobs, especially for women. Now with increasing privatization and the shrinking of state welfare, public sector jobs are disappearing. This particular route to job creation can, for all practical purposes, be treated as closed. That leaves mainly the neoliberal strategy of job creation through 'flexibility', in other words low-paid, contingent and non-standard jobs in the private sector.

Thus far only Anglo-Saxon countries, with the United States in the lead, have taken this route. Continental Europe, where unemployment is now endemic, has still to come up with an effective response to the problem. True, Japan is still clinging to its own version of full employment, one which is not, however, an easy export. But how long Japan can hold out remains to be seen. This is not to deny that some Western countries have been able to maintain low rates of unemployment. Moreover, rates of unemployment vary a great deal among industrialized countries. Nonetheless, what is clear is that Keynesian policies of economic management and stimulation, as well as the creation of public sector employment – two main pillars of the full employment policy of the golden age – have retreated in the face of globalization.[1] Given the openness of economies and the accent on post-Fordism, it is unlikely that the problem of unemployment and/or basic income for the working-age population can be solved within the Keynesian or social democratic paradigm.

Proposition 2

Globalization results in an increasing inequality in wages and working conditions through greater labour market flexibility, a differentiated 'post-Fordist' work-force and decentralized collective bargaining. Global competition and mobility of capital result in 'social dumping' and a downward shift in wages and working conditions.

This proposition receives more support from the Anglo-Saxon world than from Continental Europe or Japan. True, Japan has had a more flexible and differentiated labour market and decentralized form of collective bargaining. But so far there has not been any marked shift in inequality. Indeed comparative evidence suggests that the pattern of labour market development in English-speaking countries may best be considered as *one* among a range of feasible responses to greater economic internationalization and global competition.

As Germany, for example, shows, a dynamic and competitive economy is apparently quite compatible with a well-regulated labour market, centralized collective bargaining, high wages, good working conditions and strongly entrenched workers' rights. Indeed these conditions make for co-operative labour relations and consensus-based implementation of workplace processes which have proven highly effective in terms of efficiency and competitiveness (Streeck, 1993, pp. 146–7; Hutton, 1995a, pp. 262–8). By contrast the neoliberal approach prevalent in Anglo-Saxon countries relies on low wages, poor working conditions and insecurity of employment as the basis of competitiveness and efficiency. As an ILO study points out, there are different routes to 'flexibility', competitiveness and higher productivity. This is demonstrated by 'three of the world's most successful economies, the US, Japan and Germany ... who have very different kinds of labour markets and labour relations' (ILO, 1995, p. 19). Indeed there are many other rich industrial countries that appear to be quite successful economically without having to take the neoliberal route to the labour market.

Moreover the economic performance of countries like the UK or New Zealand, which have carried out neoliberal reforms, has not been particularly impressive. What is more evident is that neoliberal restructuring of the labour market results in the redistribution of income and power upwards. And this may provide a clue to the rationale behind this type of restructuring. It is a way of redistributing wealth and power upwards and breaking the cohesion and strength of labour which became institutionalized during the post-WW2 decades. In short, class interest drives the process which is legitimized with reference to global competition and efficiency.

However the 'logic' of labour market changes has also to do with 'social dumping'. Here the argument is that mobile capital will choose to invest in jurisdictions with low wages, lower standards of regulation and greater labour market flexibility. As a result countries will be compelled to adjust their wages and working conditions downwards. However, as we saw in Chapter 2 this argument ignores the fact that many other factors beside low wages and lack of regulation influence the decision of industry to locate. By and large these factors tend to favour location in rich industrialized countries. Moreover, what matters is not the absolute level of wages but the unit cost of production, i.e. wages in relation to productivity. This trade-off enables a high-wage and highly regulated system to be also highly productive and competitive. Hence what we find is chiefly an outflow of capital from one developed country to another rather than to low-wage countries of the Third World. True, other things being equal, capital might prefer to operate in a low-wage, low-regulation environment. And this makes some of the East European countries as well as Britain, for example, attractive for industrial investment.

It is important to keep in mind, however, that in advanced industrial countries it is not manufacturing but services that now constitute the main economic activity and source of employment. By their very nature services are difficult to locate overseas, although some parts of services operation, e.g. computing or data processing, could be located offshore. Clearly social dumping cannot be ruled out as a possible development. But it is best to see globalization as creating the conditions – by way of cross-national mobility and general empowerment of capital – in which the threat of relocation or disinvestment can be used effectively to push down wages and working conditions in developed countries. Social dumping, therefore, appears more as an aspect of industrial relations and managerial ideology than a functionally driven imperative of a global economy.

Thus far evidence for social dumping in Continental Europe is limited although as we have noted, pressures are building up, for example in Germany, for a move in this direction. We would argue that there is no *economic* compulsion stemming from globalization that requires extensive labour market deregulation and the weakening of union power that we see in the US and other Anglo-Saxon countries. While some measure of labour market deregulation and wage inequality may be necessary for the post-Fordist global economy, these stop far short of the nature and extent of changes that have occurred in Anglo-Saxon countries.

Proposition 3

Globalization exerts a downward pressure on systems of social protection and social expenditure by prioritizing the reduction of deficits and debts and the lowering of taxation as key objectives of state policy.

Undoubtedly, the mobility of capital and finance, flexible exchange rates and the ascendancy of financial markets has strengthened the hand of business and neoliberals hugely in their demand for fiscal rectitude. Since budget deficits and accumulated debt mean continued borrowing, the credit rating of governments is playing an important part in disciplining 'profligate' governments and pressuring them into reducing the deficit and debt. In any case, 'offending' governments can hardly ignore a run on their currency – a sudden crisis brought about by the flight of finance capital. And financial markets strongly favour the elimination of budget deficits and moving towards a balanced budget.

Governments can reduce or eliminate deficits in a number of ways, for example by reducing public expenditure or increasing taxes. However, the latter is strictly out of favour with investors and financial markets, who want governments to reduce not only deficits but also taxes. The mobility of finance and capital and the privileging of the market and enterprise culture result in a downward pressure on taxation. As we have seen in the case of Sweden, for example, industrialists threatened disinvestment to prevent taxes being raised. True, wide variations continue in the level of taxation among OECD countries. Moreover, taxes as a proportion of national income (GDP) show a decline in only a few high-tax countries, e.g. Sweden, over the last decade. As we have seen, in part this is because governments find it difficult to retrench social expenditure for fear of political repercussions. But it is also due to greater demand for social expenditure resulting from higher unemployment, declining or stagnant wages as well as demographic changes, e.g. an ageing population and an increase in one-parent households. Thus we find globalization having a contradictory effect on social expenditure. On the one hand it is exerting a downward pressure on social expenditure and the social state. On the other hand the deregulation and the commodification of the labour market is exerting an upward pressure on social expenditure via the compensatory mechanisms of social protection.

The pattern of financing has changed, however. Governments have reduced taxes substantially on higher incomes, lowered taxes on corporations and shifted the tax burden downwards by increasing consumption taxes and social insurance contributions. It is a tribute to the popularity of social programmes that despite a high burden of taxation, the vast majority of people in Western industrialized countries want governments not only to maintain but to improve mainstream programmes, e.g. health care, pensions and education, and are apparently willing to pay *more* in taxes to ensure this.

It is possible, however, that with the further integration of national economies in the world market, we could see renewed pressure for a downward harmonization of taxes. Employers have been complaining about payroll taxes and may want these reduced further. That could weaken the national insurance approach to social protection. Meanwhile, as we have seen, IGOs such as the OECD and IMF are actively promoting the policy of lower taxation on the grounds of reducing disincentives to work and investment and preventing market 'distortions' more generally. These IGOs are adding to the pressures stemming from business and financial sectors for keeping taxes down.

Moreover agencies such as the OECD are also involved in influencing the direction of social policy in member countries. For example they favour greater selectivity in social provision. Economic policies of regional associations such as the EU are also weighted heavily in the direction of fiscal conservatism. As we saw, the convergence criteria of the EMU on deficits have already led to significant cuts in social expenditure as countries scrambled to meet the criteria by the deadline date for joining the EMU. And although in the event the stringent Maastricht criteria were relaxed to allow member states to qualify, countries are nonetheless expected to make progress towards the fiscal standards of the EMU and to maintain fiscal discipline in the future. Policies of downward tax harmonization, if adopted by the EU, could further reinforce the trend towards the containment and reduction of state welfare.

It remains the case, however, that the effect of this downward pressure on state welfare is indirect and long term. Despite pressures stemming from globalization, nation states still have considerable autonomy in matters of fiscal and social policy. As we have seen, there are counter-pressures stemming from public opinion, electoral politics, organized interests as well as demographic and other factors which help to sustain systems of social protection built in the past and prevent the reduction of social expenditure. And although it is reassuring to think of the future of social protection in terms of 'welfare pluralism', we have to remember that neoliberalism and globalization are also weakening some of the alternative bases of social support. Thus in a competitive world with a tendency towards increasing unemployment, job insecurity and non-standard forms of work, occupational welfare cannot be expected to fill the gap left by state withdrawal. If corporations are engaged in ruthless competition world-wide then the 'Japanization' of welfare is no longer a feasible option. Moreover, apart from charitable donations of the ultra-rich, 'civil society' is not likely to have substantial fiscal capacity. Thus 'welfare pluralism', somewhat in the manner of the 'deinstitutionalization' of care in the 1970s could turn out to be a euphemism for 'Do It Yourself' social care with the extra burden falling on women. Taken together, Propositions 2 and 3 suggest that in a commodifying and globalizing economy, the state may have to take more rather than less responsibility for social protection.

Proposition 4

Globalization weakens the ideological underpinning of social protection, especially that of a national minimum, by undermining national solidarity and legitimizing inequality of rewards.

A basic principle guiding the development of the post-WW2 welfare state has been that of a national minimum standard of living below which no one should be allowed to fall. This national minimum was to be in the nature of a right of all citizens – virtually a function of citizenship or membership of the national community. The idea was to emphasize the radical break from the charitable status and limited population coverage of social programmes in the past. The welfare state itself has been very much a national enterprise fuelled by nationalistic aspirations and the desire for national integration. In place of a nation divided and weakened by class and regional inequalities, the welfare state was to create one nation united on the basis of social citizenship. It was this sense of a national community and its membership that provided much of the incentive to abolish poverty and reduce inequality.

Globalization is weakening the cohesion of the nation state by denationalizing the economy, or at any rate decentring the nation state as an economic unit. If the global market becomes the reference point and corporations feel no loyalty to the nation state as they scour the earth for the most profitable place of investment and the least costly labour force, the nation as a unit is weakened and compromised. If economic elites feel less interested in issues of national integration the 'one nation' concept underlying the welfare state is weakened. Indeed the pre-eminence of the market economy, the imperative of profit maximization and enterprise culture more generally have legitimized economic inequalities of an order that seemed scarcely possible only a decade or so ago.

True, nations differ a great deal in this regard. It is above all in the neoliberal regimes of Anglo-Saxon countries that the trend towards inequality is most pronounced. In much of Continental Europe and Japan the picture is different. But as we have argued, the trend line is not dissimilar. Inequality is creeping upwards. The commitment to nation and national community appears vulnerable as business is freed of national restrictions and obligations and as social partnership institutions decline in many countries. True, in Western Europe generally and within the EU in particular, there is a commitment to combat poverty and social exclusion. Moreover, in the 1980s at least, poverty rates do not show an upward trend in most EU countries. On the other hand as we have noted, the single economic market, the European monetary union and other economic developments within the EU, together with globalization pressures and trends could weaken systems of social protection.

It should also be noted that the idea of redistributing life-chances through progressive taxation and social benefits was a part of the post-WW2 reorganization of the welfare state, although it was social democracy that had a stronger ideological and political commitment to the goal of redistribution. To some extent both the security and the equity objectives of the welfare state were a response to the systemic challenge of socialism – from within in the form of socialist movements and parties, and from without in the form of state socialist societies. Egalitarianism and redistribution were thus connected with the objectives of ameliorating class conflict and responding to demands for social justice – in short with the legitimation problems of capitalism.

These redistributive objectives of the welfare state seem to have dropped out of political discourse as has the objective of economic equality more generally. Globalization and the retreat of the socialist alternative have put paid to these egalitarian objectives of the welfare state. This is not to deny that a substantial amount of *horizontal* redistribution as well as short-term vertical redistribution does take place through tax-transfer systems generally. Overall, however, globalization seems to be acting as a strong force in favour of inequality of income and wealth distribution.

Proposition 5

Globalization weakens the basis of social partnership and tripartism by shifting the balance of power away from labour and the state and towards capital.

Perhaps in common with Proposition 1 on full employment, this proposition is unlikely to be controversial. The openness of economies has undermined the conditions in which business, labour and government could negotiate various economic trade-offs. Thus organized labour offered wage moderation and accepted new technologies and work processes in exchange for full employment, economic growth and social welfare.

Governments can no longer deliver full employment and economic growth. At the same time capital is less in need of labour co-operation. In conditions of unemployment and cross-national mobility of capital, it can obtain labour compliance through the market mechanism. As a result in some countries such as Sweden, social partnership and tripartism have been weakened a great deal, if not undermined. On the other hand, elsewhere, e.g. Germany, Austria and Norway, neocorporatist institutions and practices remain in place. Although in structural terms capital finds itself in a stronger position in relation to labour as well as government, there are other factors that influence the continuation or otherwise of social partnership arrangements (Huber and Stephens, 1998; Garrett, 1998, Chapter 6).

We would hypothesize that other things being equal, the degree of international orientation and centralization of firms may be an important variable influencing capital's withdrawal from social partnership institutions. For example it is well known that Swedish capital is far more internationalized and centralized than Norwegian capital, and this may be part of the explanation of why the two countries differ in respect of social partnership. The state of the economy may be another important variable. Arguably the continuation of German neocorporatism has been made possible by Germany's economic success as a nation as well as German capital's greater national orientation. Globalization brings about a structural shift in the distribution of power between capital and labour. But the exact institutional implications and the behaviour of the collective actors concerned depend on various mediating factors.

We must remember, too, that the model of organized co-operation between major social actors has many positive features associated with it. Social partnership arrangements could conceivably continue in favourable national settings in order to manage change through consensus, even if objectives such as full employment and economic growth can no longer be attained in this way. The ideological orientation of governments is also important. Whereas neoliberal governments are likely to dismantle neocorporatist institutions in favour of market relationships, conservative corporatist as well as social-democratic governments are likely to try to maintain these arrangements. Globalization pressures are invariably refracted through national institutions and specific national conditions. In short the logic of the global–national relationship is not linear but 'dialectical' or interactive.

Proposition 6
Globalization constrains the policy options of nations by virtually excluding left-of-centre approaches. In this sense it spells the 'end of
ideology' as far as welfare state policies are concerned.

As we have seen there are substantial and continuing differences in the
approaches, policies and outcomes concerning the welfare state between
Anglo-Saxon countries on the one hand and those of Continental Europe and
Japan on the other. Put simply, the former lean far more towards a neoliberal
approach as evident in their social policies and outcomes. In countries outside the Anglo-Saxon world, on the other hand, the post-WW2 'social contract'
between capital and labour and between the citizen and the state remains far
more intact (even though full employment has gone).

Moreover, even within the Anglo-Saxon group there are significant differences in approaches to social policy, e.g. between Australia and New Zealand
or the US and Canada. These differences have to do, at least in part, with
choices made by the government in office. As Castles (1996) and Castles and
Pierson (1998) point out, Australia and New Zealand have chosen very different modes of adjustment to the changing international economic environment.
Clearly politics matter and it would be absurd to claim that globalization
pressures exclude choice altogether. But what kind of choice? Essentially
what we are concerned with here is the question of a narrowing of the range
of options, the *limits* within which choice is exercised rather than the question of choice *per se*, i.e. economic determinism versus political choice. The
question then is *how much* do party politics matter today as far as welfare
state policies are concerned? And what difference has globalization made to
the 'politics matter' thesis? And what are the implications? These are some of
the questions that need to be asked and answered more specifically than has
been possible in this exploratory study.

More particularly, the above proposition asserts that 'left-of-centre' approaches to social policy are virtually excluded. But what do we mean by a
'left-of-centre' approach? We refer to a policy orientation that involves the
following: (i) the expansion rather than contraction of the public sector –
whether in respect of state responsibility for social protection, the ownership
or control of economic enterprises or the regulation of the national economy;
(ii) the extension of progressive and redistributive taxation; (iii) the maintenance or restoration of full employment; (iv) the reduction of income and
wage differentials; (v) greater universality rather than selectivity in social
programmes.

In short, by 'left' policies we mean more scope for the public sector in
maintaining social standards and more equality of income and conditions
among citizens and regions. Thus we may distinguish between (i) 'right' or

neoliberal, (ii) 'progressive' or liberal/centrist (the 'third way' or the 'afford-able' welfare state?) and (iii) 'left' social policies. New Zealand represents the first group, Australia the second and Norway the third. In addition, there is a fourth approach – the conservative corporatist – of which Germany and Japan may be considered as two cultural variants. Of these it is the 'left' approach that has lost credibility, economically and politically, in the 1990s. Why? Essentially because of the integration of national economies in the global market and capital mobility, but also because of the ideological as-cendancy of neoliberalism and the absence of a left-of-centre model of macroeconomic management. Again we have to point out that these policy orientations are ideal types. The policies of governments and countries are often a mix, and it is partly a question of the dominant trait or tendency.

In any case what seems to be happening in many European countries, including the Scandinavian, is more a matter of maintaining the institutional legacy of the past than initiating new policies.[2] This is particularly the case with social policies of the Left. No wonder welfare states, especially outside the Anglo-Saxon world, exhibit a 'frozen landscape' (Esping-Andersen, 1996a, p. 24). True, we have seen some developments on the Left lately, for example the election of the Socialist Government of L. Jospin in France, which sug-gest a departure from the centre-right orientations now typical of social democracy. However, although the Jospin Government was elected on a platform with a left orientation, it came to power in the wake of a strong protest movement which included industrial action against the austerity poli-cies of the previous government. Secondly, although the Government has made some progress, it remains to be seen whether and to what extent it succeeds in carrying out its electoral promises. For the moment, then, the jury is still out on the Jospin Government and on the wider significance of recent developments in France.

The phrase 'end of ideology' may sound like a resurrection of the techno-logical and economic determinism fashionable in the 1960s. But the point is that the broad policy consensus, i.e. what is politically feasible, has shifted to the right. Globalization and the demise of a left alternative are important factors behind this shift. Whether the virtual exclusion of a left-of-centre approach should be called the end of ideology or not is, of course, debatable. As some commentators have argued, the apparent lack of choice and help-lessness of national governments in the face of external pressures from financial markets and other sources serve as a convenient rationalization for neoliberal policies. Thus globalization becomes a means of 'blame avoidance' for politi-cians carrying out unpopular policies.

This is true but does not make globalization a 'myth'. It may be difficult if not impossible to separate the 'objective' elements of constraint that stem from capital mobility and financial openness from the 'subjective' or ideological elements. The latter refer to the representation of globalization as inevitable, uncontrollable, beneficial and driven by impersonal market forces, etc., and its use by the media, politicians and corporate interests as a convenient legitimation for neoliberal policies. However, the determined struggle waged by social democratic governments in countries such as Sweden to defend full employment and social citizenship shows the harsh economic reality of globalization, i.e. of being held hostage by financial markets and mobile capital, which cannot be wished away. In other countries the confrontation has been less direct, but the fact that with one or two notable exceptions, social democratic parties are unwilling or unable to maintain a left-of-centre policy stance should make us wary of the claim that globalization is a myth, an imaginary 'cult of impotence' to which left politicians and disenchanted intellectuals have subscribed too readily.

Thus a Canadian defender of the welfare state asserts that: 'the obstacles preventing us from gaining control over our economic lives have little to do with globalization and technology. The real obstacle is political' (McQuaig, 1998, p. 26). Governments can fight unemployment effectively and finance social programmes adequately but don't do it. Why? Because 'they have chosen to render themselves impotent, powerless in the face of the capital markets' (ibid.). Thus it all boils down to a 'failure of the will on the part of governments', including social democratic governments who are keen to adopt 'the market agenda once they've attained power' (ibid., p. 28). However, despite the sincerity of these pronouncements and the strong feelings behind them, they cannot substitute for an adequate analysis of the state we are in and what can be done to change it, i.e. the constraints as well as opportunities at the present time.

Hirst and Thompson take a similar albeit more qualified view of the situation. They write: 'One key effect of the concept of globalization has been to paralyse radical reforming national strategies, to see them as unviable in the face of the judgment and sanction of international markets' (1996, p. 1). They try to demonstrate that, contrary to what many globalists claim, the process of globalization is not very advanced, that the economic changes taking place are more 'complex and equivocal', and that there is more scope for 'national and international control of market economies in order to promote social goals' (ibid., p. 2). Nonetheless they acknowledge that greater internationalization of economies has imposed 'constraints on certain types of national economic strategy' (ibid., p. 4). More recently Garrett (1998) has argued that globalization notwithstanding, social democratic corporatism remains a viable option for combining economic efficiency with equity and distributive justice. As we pointed out earlier (see Chapter 1, note 2) Garrett's thesis suffers from some major weaknesses. One of these is his failure to consider the implications of the enhanced power and opportunities of capital as a result of the openness of economies. He overestimates (i) the capacity of social corporatism to deliver labour market 'flexibility', economic efficiency, wage moderation and low inflation, and (ii) the willingness of capital to accept the constraints of corporatism (see Garrett, 1998, Chapter 6).

Nonetheless global sceptics are right in challenging the strong versions of global determinism. National governments can and do make different policy choices. Modest forms of social corporatism which deliver more equitable trade-offs between equity and efficiency are and can remain viable, especially in countries with a long history of successful corporatism. The main point at issue is the rightward shift in the range of feasible policies. Global sceptics fail to provide convincing arguments or evidence (except by way of the historical continuity of past patterns in a few small nations such as Norway) that left-of-centre policies (as defined above) remain possible in conditions of globalization. One problem with global sceptics' approach is to see globalization almost exclusively in economic terms. As we have argued in this book, the collapse of communism and the fading of the socialist vision of an alternative society form the essential context of globalization. Any assessment of the prospects for left policies today must take into account the ideological and political as well as the economic aspects of globalization

Proposition 7

The logic of globalization comes into conflict with the 'logic' of the national community and democratic politics. Social policy emerges as a major issue of contention between global capitalism and the democratic nation state.

The thrust of globalization is towards the denationalization of economies by making them more open to transnational economic activities in search of profits and higher returns. Globalization is about turning the whole world into a giant market place where national boundaries mean, or should mean, little.

Needless to say this is more a distant goal than present-day reality. As we argued earlier (Chapter 1), the distinction between the internationalization of economies and their globalization is a useful one, but the two can be seen as points on a scale. The process of globalization involves moving the world economy further along the route to a 'borderless world'. The MAI for example, if and when implemented, would be a major step in this direction. Recall that its main objective is to further the rights of MNCs and other foreign investors against the autonomy of national governments to impose restrictions on foreign investors. The MAI has been aptly described as the global investors' charter. There are other examples of how the process is being moved forward, e.g. through conditions imposed by the IMF on debtor nations and through the rules and regulations of the WTO.

No doubt in principle the objectives of globalization, i.e. freer trade between nations and freer movement of money and capital, freer communication and flow of information are entirely beneficial. But here is the problem. Like national market economies, the global market economy also requires regulation. At the national level we have properly constituted and democratically elected governments to decide how far and in what respect the economy should be regulated.

However there is no properly constituted global government, no democratically elected international authority that has both the capacity and legitimacy to *regulate* globalization and to ensure that it works fairly and in the broad interest of the people. Much of today's globalization is entirely unregulated, for example the financial flows between nations, or regulated in the interest of business and capital, for example intellectual property rights prescribed by the WTO. More specifically, there seems to be a large gap in *social regulation* at the global level, i.e. in respect of the prescription of basic social standards concerning health and safety in the workplace, employment protection, income security, health, education and other social services.

There is a parallel of sorts between today's globalization and the advance of a market economy in the 19th century, for example in Britain, with its thrust towards the deregulation of existing systems of economic and social protection and the promotion of *laissez-faire*. Moreover, the parallel extends to the political dimension in that the mass of the people remained disfranchised in the 19th century and decisions were made by the economic and political elites. It was only with the democratization of the nation state that the market economy was regulated with reference to the interests of the mass of people.

Today we are faced with a situation where national economies have become far more open and internationalized, but the site for democratic regulation of economic activity remains the nation state.[3] Thus there is an inevitable conflict between the demands of a globalizing process seeking to establish (in the ideal-typical sense) universal *laissez-faire* with scant regard for its social and human (including environmental) consequences, and the democratic nation state with its mandate of collective responsibility for the well-being of the national community, a mandate largely institutionalized through systems of social protection. It is these that face the prospect of erosion through the neoliberal thrust of globalization, which would make the market sovereign. Hence as we saw earlier (Chapter 4), the fight for the defence of social protection on the part of the electorate, interest groups and social movements.

No doubt national politicians face a difficult situation. Globalizing elites and the IGOs involved in promoting globalization want national governments to act as facilitators and promoters of the globalization process within their jurisdictions. Put simply, their role is to 'sell' the policies favoured by globalizers to their citizens. A variety of arguments and strategies are available for the purpose, e.g. that such policies are in the best interests of the nation's economy, that there are no viable alternatives, that short-term pain will bring long-term gain, etc.

One particularly effective strategy is to orchestrate a 'crisis', e.g. to raise an alarm about debts and deficits ballooning 'out of control', with the nation facing desertion by international lenders and investors and the like. A timely warning by the IMF to the country to put its financial house in order or a hint by bond-rating agencies that the government's credit rating may be downgraded are helpful in strengthening the politician's hand against the electorate. It might be useful to distinguish between politicians of the Right, who may be active promoters of globalization and who might *initiate* policies of deregulation, deficit cutting, tax reduction, etc., and others who find themselves between the Scylla of responding to the demands of globalizers and corporations and the Charybdis of being responsive to the demands of the electorate. Thus a simple conceptualization of the global market and the nation state as conflicting entities is misleading in so far as right-wing national governments may be active promoters of globalization and also in so far as the globalization process itself has to work through the compliance and consent of the national government. However, to the extent that there is an electoral democracy in place, national governments of all kinds have to respond to the demands of the electorate for maintaining systems of social protection. In this sense there is an inherent conflict between globalization, which is transnational and undemocratic and democracy, which is rooted in the nation state.

But why is social policy a major issue of contention between the forces of global capitalism and the democratic nation state? There are several overlapping reasons. Post-WW2 social policy or the welfare state has been about decommodifying labour and life-chances more generally. Measures such as full employment, employment protection, unemployment benefits, minimum wage laws, health and safety legislation and trade union rights institutionalize basic social standards and to that extent, limit the scope of the market. From the perspective of creating a global market economy, these regulations appear as so many impediments which prevent the deployment of labour freely as a commodity. Moreover they 'distort' the price of labour. In a globally competitive but unregulated environment, competitive advantage appears to lie with 'flexible' labour markets. Hence the emphasis on removing these 'rigidities' in the name of becoming more competitive.

No matter what the euphemism employed, the fact remains that what appears from the viewpoint of the global economy as an impediment to be removed appears from the viewpoint of a national community as the humanization of conditions of life and work for all citizens, thus giving tangible meaning to the idea of community in the national setting. It is also important to bear in mind that systems of social protection represent the outcome of more than a century of struggle in which democratic political rights have played a major part. Not surprisingly, then, the attempt on the part of capital to undo these gains of democratic struggle by denationalizing the economy and thus moving economic policy beyond the pale of democratic decision-making appears as a major, if covert and indirect, assault on democracy. Globalization is not only threatening to roll back the welfare state; given its unregulated and undemocratic character, it is also threatening to roll back democracy. As a result there is a double deficit emerging – a social as well as a democratic deficit. Hence the conflict over social policy between the forces of globalism and those of national democracy.

Who is winning the battle? Let us say the situation is one of stalemate, even though globalizers have made significant inroads into social protection, especially in Anglo-Saxon countries. Current tensions and frustrations around social policy are an expression of the democratic deficit arising out of a situation where the nation state has lost some of its sovereignty and autonomy, but there is no democracy as yet at the supranational level which can restore people's 'voice' at that level.

The growing asymmetry between the economic and political realms can, in principle, be dealt with in a number of ways. One option is to reverse the process of financial globalization and restore capital controls and other mechanisms in place earlier, thus giving back the nation state its lost sovereignty (Bienenfeld, 1994). The political feasibility of such a turnabout remains doubtful. However, emerging contradictions of global capitalism such as the serious destabilization of economies resulting from financial openness may help to bring this about.

A second option is to accept greater internationalization and globalization, but to ensure that the process is *democratically regulated* and socially responsible. The problem with this option is the absence of democratic institutions of global governance. These cannot be created overnight. Indeed, despite many schemes of reform of global governance, the practical difficulties of creating democratic institutions that will function effectively at the international level are, at the moment, overwhelming.

A third option would be for progressive social movements and parties, in the developed world at any rate, to come together in formulating the principles and guidelines of a regulated globalization and forcing the hand of the global economic elite. This may represent a viable third way – between renationalizing the global economy and leaving it largely unregulated, as at present. Strong political action at both national and international levels may succeed in placing some restrictions on globalization – the Tobin Tax for example belongs here – to ensure financial stability and social protection.[4] But how feasible is it? This is too large a question to be considered in this book. At any rate as the history of capitalism shows, the self-destructing tendency of an unregulated market economy does eventually compel some measure of regulation. Indeed the current (1998) crisis of the global economy could be the catalyst for such a regulatory development.[5]

It is also important to remind ourselves that globalization is not a 'natural' phenomenon that has simply evolved out of the decline of Keynesianism. Removal of capital controls, free trade and investment, floating exchange rates and other forms of deregulation are the result of deliberate actions of Western economic elites following the disarray of Keynesianism. Indeed it is a process which is being extended and consolidated through the decisions of the G7 and other influential IGOs, e.g. the IMF and OECD. Globalization, in other words, is a phenomenon which is at once economic, political and ideological. Thus it can be opposed, regulated or reversed by political action. But in practice national governments, acting on their own and within the confines of Western economic and political institutions, are likely to achieve only limited success. There is also the possibility of a protectionist and national–chauvinist response.[6]

Thus concerted action is needed at the international level in order to underwrite systems of social protection and thus ensure the openness of economies. In the next and final chapter we look beyond the nation state and consider the problem of moving towards transnational social standards.

NOTES

1. Even Garrett, a redoubtable defender of the viability of a social democratic approach in conditions of internationalization, seems to concede this. He advocates labour market policies and other supply side strategies, e.g. education and training to counter unemployment (Garrett, 1998, pp. 28, 145–6). See also Huber and Stephens (1998) for the prospects of a social democratic approach to unemployment through a mix of supply side and other policies.
2. An exception to this seems to be the long-term care programme, based on social insurance, for the aged. First legislated by Germany in 1994, it has been followed by Japan in 1997. Child care and elderly care are two areas of social provision where we may see some state initiatives. It should be noted, however, that the German programme, though nominally funded by equal contribution of employees and employers, is in effect funded by the former. The Japanese scheme is apparently cost-shared between the insured individual and the state rather than employers, no doubt to relieve the latter of the burden of additional labour costs (on Germany see Gotting et al., 1994; on Japan see Okamoto, 1998).
3. Among supranational organizations involved in regulating economic and social activities, perhaps the EU comes closest to a quasi-democratic body. Others range between for example the IMF, with voting strength based explicitly on the economic power of nations, and the nominally 'democratic' WTO where each nation state has one vote.
4. A small tax (0.5 per cent or less) on all foreign exchange transactions was proposed by Nobel laureate James Tobin in 1978. It is meant to discourage short-term speculation without interfering with trade-related or productive investments. The Tobin Tax has attracted a great deal of interest world-wide. See ul Haq et al. (1996) and Dillon (1997).

5. The vulnerability of economies, especially those of developing countries as a result of financial openness, has been underlined dramatically after the currency crisis in East Asian countries in 1997. The 'domino' effect on Russia and Latin America and on stock markets throughout the world became evident in 1998. The fear that Western economies could be seriously affected by these developments has made the international climate much more favourable to some measure of regulation. National control on capital movements – considered a heresy by global economic orthodoxy until recently – is now being seen in these circles as not only feasible but almost desirable (Elliott, 1998, p. 19; *Financial Post*, 1998, p. C5).

6. Rieger and Leibfried (1998) argue that by cushioning sections of society from the adverse effects of globalization, the welfare state can help to prevent a protectionist and nationalist backlash. It can thus act as an ally of internationalization and free trade.

7. Towards a global social policy

Previous chapters were concerned with the logic of globalization and its implications for welfare states. In this chapter we look beyond the nation state – at the problems and prospects of social policy in a world where economies are becoming more and more internationalized. The earlier chapters were largely descriptive or 'positive' in orientation; this final chapter is more prescriptive and normative. It also returns to some of the broader themes connected with globalization outlined in the opening chapter, notably the collapse of the socialist alternative and the decentring of the nation state.

SOCIAL POLICY AFTER SOCIALISM

As we argued in Chapter 1, the collapse of the socialist alternative is for us the essential context for the resurgence of economic globalization. Let us remind ourselves briefly of the significance of socialism for social welfare. From the perspective of social policy, socialism may be seen as an attempt to solve some of the root causes of social problems endemic in capitalist society, namely economic insecurity, deprivation and inequality. Socialism locates the source of the problem at the structural or fundamental level, i.e. in private ownership of the means of production and the market economy. A socialized economy with popular control over the distribution of incomes and other resources could, it was believed, solve the problem of distributive justice at a structural level – a problem addressed by social policy in a market society largely at the level of symptoms. Such at any rate was the premise, and promise, of socialism. While socialists differed in what they believed was the route to socialist society – Marxists choosing the revolutionary road and social democrats the evolutionary road – their goals were broadly similar. The state socialist societies that came into being in Russia, Eastern Europe and elsewhere after WW1 and the social democratic movement in the West which sought to change capitalist societies from within through the ballot box, represent attempts to realize these goals.

From the vantage point of the 1990s, i.e. after the collapse of communism and the retreat of advanced social democracies such as Sweden from the socialist path, it is clear that the idea of a historically conditioned 'final' solution to some of the most enduring problems centred in the relationship between the economy and society was mistaken. The 'end of history' thesis elaborated by Fukuyama (1992) and others celebrates this fact. However, the failure of communism as a social system does not necessarily mean the failure of socialist ideas and objectives tout court. Indeed social democracy, which sought to pursue these objectives through incremental reform, has not only not been a failure, rather it has been highly successful.

The project of advanced social democracies, namely that of regulating the market economy so as to combine equity with efficiency, security with enterprise and individual freedom with a measure of social solidarity and community was very successful. The three decades after WW2 – the golden age of welfare capitalism – saw the flowering of the mixed economy and the welfare state, especially in Western Europe. Scandinavian countries perhaps best represent the development of a social democratic version of welfare capitalism which created societies that must be regarded as among the best the world has seen. Among other things, the redress of gender inequality – despite important limitations – may be singled out as one of the notable achievements of the Scandinavian welfare states (Harding, 1998). The virtual abolition of poverty among the aged in Sweden must also be recognized as a historic achievement.[1]

To be sure social-democratic reforms fell far short of what might be considered as the realization of the socialist vision. Moreover, as we have seen, the Scandinavian model of a mixed economy and the welfare state has run into problems – problems which have to do with globalization or the denationalization of economies (see pp. 75–80). But as a social system which combined efficiency with social justice and democracy, the post-WW2 welfare state represents a resounding success, not a failure. Indeed if there is a 'winner' in the contest between the three social systems of *laissez-faire* capitalism, state socialism and welfare capitalism or the mixed economy and the welfare state, it is surely the last of the three. For whereas *laissez-faire* capitalism led to the cataclysm of the 1930s followed by a world war, and state socialism to political tyranny and economic failure, welfare capitalism managed to create a stable and balanced society encapsulating some of the best features of modernity.

The political right celebrates the triumph of capitalism by contrasting it with the failures of state socialism. With the demise of state socialism, however, the more relevant comparison is between the two major variants of capitalism: *laissez-faire* and social market or welfare capitalism. As the 'welfare' or the 'social' element of post-WW2 welfare capitalism is scaled back, notably in English-speaking countries such as the UK, the US and New Zealand, we are once again beginning to see the inevitable consequences of *laissez-faire* capitalism, namely increasing inequality and polarization, growing insecurity and poverty, and social degradation (see Chapter 2). Thus an important question to ask is what kind of capitalism is it that has won and what kind of socialism that has lost?

Not only do the apologists of capital proclaim liberal capitalism as the victor, critics on the Left do the same. The former applaud the victory, the latter bemoan it. And some ideologues on the Left fail to see any difference between the different kinds of capitalisms. Thus from a neo-Marxist stand-point Teeple (1995b, p. 43) writes: 'Even if it can be argued that the actions of social democracy made for a more comprehensive welfare state, necessary and valuable for the working class as a whole ... the KWS did not constitute a transformed capitalism, and the vaunted "redistribution" of wealth has always been very limited'. True, social democracy did not bring about a structural transformation of capitalism into socialism. But one wonders how useful it is to judge 'actually existing' social systems in relation to some ideal society that exists only in the imagination of social theorists.

Perhaps it is also important to remind ourselves that socialism ought to be voluntary – freely chosen by the people – rather than imposed on the masses by an ideological elite. Once the notion of 'false consciousness' and the theory of a political vanguard is abandoned, then the need for a consensus-based or at least a majoritarian approach to social change becomes essential. It may well be that ecological damage and degradation will compel a radical retreat from the mindless growth and abject consumerism of advanced capitalist societies. For the moment, however, a systemic alternative to, or a radical paradigm shift from, the consumerist society is not in sight. At a minimum therefore it is necessary to prevent the dismantling of the welfare state and a return to something like the *laissez-faire* capitalism of pre-war days. The welfare state may not amount to socialism but as Teeple and other fundamentalists grudgingly concede, universal social programmes are largely the product of people's struggle against the insecurities and inequities of a free market society. They represent, however imperfectly, the values of community, solidarity and the recognition of human need within the confines of a market economy. They need defending against the depredations of a globalizing capitalism.

It must also be pointed out that neo-Marxists and other 'systemic' thinkers on the Left tend to overgeneralize from the experience of Anglo-Saxon countries and downplay the comparative dimension. Yet the intra-systemic differences within capitalism are important – indeed more so today than ever before, since we do not seem to have many systemic alternatives around. The distinction between European (as well as Japanese) social market capitalism and Anglo-American neoliberal capitalism cannot therefore be dismissed as trivial (Albert, 1993; Hutton, 1995a). Indeed the unregulated globalization with its tendency towards the residualization of welfare that we are witnessing today represents a neoliberal approach.

The European model of a mixed economy with its concern for equity and community differs in important ways from the neoliberal model. Yet it has proven highly efficient, dynamic and seemingly quite compatible with an internationalized economy (Albert, 1993; Hutton, 1995a). East Asian capitalism, which differs in significant ways from its European counterpart, has at least one element in common with it. It too has a social or communitarian dimension. Indeed in today's world the Anglo-Saxon form of capitalism – though pre-eminent because of the United States – represents a minority viewpoint and only a minority of people of industrialized nations live under it. The majority of people of developed nations live and work under forms of capitalism quite different from the individualistic, hyper-liberal version associated with Anglo-Saxon economies. It is important not only to acknowledge this difference, but also to note that the social market model of European capitalism represents the values of community and solidarity. It embodies, for example, the contribution and influence of organized labour and social Christianity as well as democracy. The importance of this basic social market approach as a model for connecting the economic with the social cannot be overstated. In a different cultural context and within a different configuration of values and institutions, East Asian capitalism also represents a social market approach.

Yet it also remains true that the social market model – in both the Japanese and the European variant – is under threat from globalization, which is essentially neoliberalism writ large (see Chapter 5). As we argued earlier (Chapter 5), in different ways countries as disparate as Sweden, Germany and Japan are facing the problem of adjusting and accommodating to a model of global capitalism shaped largely by the Anglo-Saxon approach. *Acting on their own*, even powerful nations such as Germany may not be able to resist the pressures (both endogenous and exogenous) for deregulation and the scaling down of standards which could result in the scuttling of the social compact. Weaker nations could face greater risk of capital flight and loss of competitiveness if they tried to go it alone in maintaining social standards.[2] The deregulation of labour markets and the scaling down of social standards (albeit restrained and limited by democracy) initiated by Anglo-Saxon countries represents social dumping on a global scale. The idea that other countries will remain unscathed and will be able to muddle along in their own way and under their own steam seems implausible in the long run.

In short, global *laissez-faire*, entrenched welfare states and electoral democracy are an unstable combination which could prove to be explosive. If ultra-nationalism and protectionism, as a backlash against unregulated globalization, are to be avoided, then some form of international action on social protection – even symbolic action at this point by say the G7 nations could be significant – is needed to complement and so to 'save' economic internationalization. National responses need to be supplemented with action at the transnational level to establish and safeguard social standards. What are the problems and prospects of developing such standards at a supranational level?

GLOBALIZATION AND SOCIAL STANDARDS: BRINGING THE 'SOCIAL' BACK IN

Our starting point must be the growing dissociation between economic and social standards in a globalizing economy. The neoliberal thrust of globalization spearheaded by American capitalism is to strengthen market forces and the economic realm at the cost of the institutions of social protection – institutions which appear as so many impediments to profit maximization. As we witness the gradual impoverishment of the 'social' in Anglo-Saxon countries, let us remind ourselves of the great achievement of the golden age of welfare capitalism represented by the welfare state and the mixed economy. It was to recognize the importance of the social dimension and to bring the social and economic sectors together in a mutually supportive, positive-sum relationship.

This harks back to a fundamental problem of the market society and market relationships with which social thinkers such as Marx, Durkheim, Toennies, Polanyi and others wrestled. Essentially it had to do with the dire consequences of the ascendancy of the 'economic' and the attenuation of the 'social' in the market-oriented societies which emerged in Europe in the 19th century. The different prognoses and remedies proposed by these theorists need not concern us here. Rather we would like to note that the long reprise of the social which began with factory legislation in Britain and continued through the development of social insurance in Germany was followed by other measures leading up to the relatively balanced social order of the post-WW2 welfare state. The latter managed to reintegrate the economic and the social within the framework of the nation state. Late 20th-century globalization is dissolving the nexus between the economic and the social as it once more exalts the economic and downgrades the 'social', seeking to relegate the latter to the private sphere.

The process of downgrading the social began with the ascendancy of neoliberalism at the nation-state level in the late 1970s. Globalization has carried the process forward by empowering and privileging neoliberal economics as a transnational force beyond the control of nation states and governments. What economic globalizers fail to acknowledge, however, is that whereas economies can go global, people cannot. While money and capital have been set free to move across the globe, labour remains locked into the nation state, for example by strict control on immigration. By and large people have to live and survive locally. Indeed human communities are defined above all by language and culture and are thus rooted in a place – a geographical location. Economies have gone global but societies and communities remain national. The result is a growing hiatus between the needs of the economic realm, e.g. for cost-cutting and profit maximization, and those of the social realm for stability, security and a sense of belongingness and cohesion. In short the logic of economic *laissez-faire* is to destroy communities and social life altogether. Hence the problem of controlling the economic in order to save the social is back on the agenda. It is necessary to affirm once again the importance of the social and to make it an integral component – alongside the economic – of development and progress.

FROM SOCIAL RIGHTS TO SOCIAL STANDARDS: A CONCEPTUAL REORIENTATION

The conceptual underpinning of the post-WW2 welfare state has been that of social rights of citizenship in a modern democratic state. Although it was the social democratic welfare state, developed most fully in Scandinavian countries, that went furthest in making social citizenship the basis of social policy, it is important to note that in virtually all Western welfare states the idea of state welfare as a 'right' or entitlement (as opposed to a form of stigmatizing charity) and as a more or less universal provision to include all citizens has been the key element which distinguishes modern from pre-war social policy. True, there were important differences among post-war welfare state regimes. But these cross-national variations have to be seen within the larger epochal shift in the conception of social policy from the pre-war to the post-war world.

Shorn of complexities, the basic shift can be summed up as that from a residual to an institutional conception of state welfare, although the latter conception found expression in a variety of sub-types, e.g. the social democratic, the conservative corporatist or Bismarckian, and the Anglo-Saxon liberal (Esping-Andersen, 1990). Be that as it may the theoretical underpinning and the normative justification of the institutional model has been the conception of social welfare as an essential institution of the modern state – expressing one of the rights of citizenship, namely social, alongside civil and political rights. In this perspective of modernization which we owe to T.H. Marshall (1950), social rights appeared in the wake of the establishment of civil and political rights, rounding off the development of citizenship in the modern democratic state. The last two decades have seen a burgeoning literature on citizenship and social rights (see for example Turner, 1986; Barbalet, 1988; Andrews, 1991; Roche, 1992). The critique, the refinements and the qualifications brought to bear on the idea of social rights in its various aspects need not concern us here. Rather the point to make is that social rights looked secure and well established during the golden age – a time when they appeared to be in a positive-sum relationship with economic and political rights. The welfare state appeared as positively beneficial for the economy and a major contributor to political stability and national integration. It was easy to see social rights as a part of the broader conception of human rights in a modern society.

Since the late 1970s, however, social rights have taken a beating, both ideologically and in practice, at least in Anglo-Saxon countries. The basic weakness of social rights as a concept is that it is not at par with the other two rights, i.e. civil and political. Whereas these two are essentially *procedural* and can be institutionalized as universal human rights, social rights are *substantive* in nature (Barry, 1990, pp. 78–81; Plant et al., 1980, pp. 71–82). They raise issues of mobilizing and redistributing material resources.[4] The bottom line is that the granting of social rights comes into conflict with economic or property rights, one of the basic rights in liberal capitalist societies. The substantive rather than procedural status of social rights meant that when Western economies ran into serious problems after the mid-1970s, it was economic or property rights that received priority. Social rights, which were seen as encroaching upon property rights, were downgraded. As a result while civil and political rights of citizenship are not a matter of contention and are being extended world-wide, social rights are on the defensive, if not in decline. Their future looks decidedly uncertain (Esping-Andersen, 1996a, p. 1).

A further problem with the concept of social welfare as a 'right' is its individual-centred nature. To claim that individuals have a right, say to an adequate income which must be granted to them from resources to which others have a duty to contribute, raises the question of individual merit, i.e. whether individuals are deserving or not and whether they have contributed in ways which entitle them to their 'right'. In short, the source of these *substantive* claims of individuals upon resources remains problematic.

Social rights are also problematic in that as substantive rights to a standard of life, they imply a *minimum* rather than an optimum standard. Yet mainstream social programmes such as pensions and health care go well beyond minimum standards and often aim at an optimum. As a result they are vulnerable to the argument that they should be reduced to a minimum (Barry, 1990, p. 80; Espada, 1996, pp. 121–3, 186–7).

Finally, the language of 'rights', especially the notion of individual rights, is largely *Western* in origin. In non-Western countries, e.g. the newly industrializing countries of East Asia, 'social rights of citizenship' mean very little. Thus the key concept of Western social welfare remains largely alien to the non-Western world (Goodman and Peng, 1996, pp. 215, 218 n.29; Jones, 1993, pp. 202, 209, 214). Yet what is valuable in the idea of social rights of welfare – and here T.H. Marshall's contribution is seminal – is the emphasis on the social or the community dimension of modern societies besides the economic and political dimensions. But the *form* in which it appears, i.e. as an *individual* right analogous to civil and political rights, is virtually unknown outside the Western tradition. In any case, faced with the challenge of property and market rights, social rights are in retreat as a normative concept. Indeed with the resurgence of the market principle and the privileging of the economic realm, the idea of social citizenship is losing credibility. True, systems of social protection still remain in place in most Western countries, but increasingly find themselves on the defensive. They survive primarily as a legacy of the past, defended by the citizenry and vested interests, but lacking a clear rationale and meaning in the new order of things. In sum the concept of social welfare needs revision – both from an ideological and theoretical standpoint and also in order to clarify the rationale of the institutions of social protection.

The first step in the renewal of the concept of social welfare is to restate its meaning and place in the development of modern industrial societies. We would argue that the 'social' dimension identified by Marshall must be seen as a universal category similar to those of the 'economic' or 'political' in modern society. The economic order is concerned with the efficient production of goods and services and the market is the key institution. The political is concerned with the mechanism of decision-making and the distribution and exercise of power. The democratic polity is the key institution. The social is concerned with the maintenance of community and social solidarity, and universal social provision is the key institution. Thus the 'community' emerges as a societal category similar to the economy and the polity. In other words we need to think in terms of *community standards* rather than *individual rights*, for it is the community as a collective that must have some social standards or norms, which entail both rights and obligations. The concept of community, like democracy and other normative concepts, is a contested one (Plant et al., 1980). But it can be argued that membership in a national community which entails reciprocity, interdependence and solidarity presupposes basic rather than minimum standards. It is the role of the polity to guarantee or uphold these basic social standards.

The notion of a community or social collective has a far wider applicability and meaning than individual 'rights' – a concept of Western provenance. Social welfare as an expression of the basic social *standards* of a community and its concern for its members can thus be universalized across different cultures and societies (Doyal and Gough, 1991, p. 223). Secondly, social standards can be linked more logically to the economic standards and capacities of nations than the more abstract and procedural notion of *rights*. The idea of a standard commensurate with the economic development of nations could help overcome the vexed problem of developed societies demanding a level of social protection and labour standards from less developed societies, which appears arbitrary and which the latter can ill afford to provide (Doyal and Gough, 1991, pp. 230–31). Finally, the idea of a social standard commensurate with economic development could help overcome the problem faced by the International Labour Organization (ILO), the United Nations (UN) and other agencies in trying to apply social rights universally across countries of differing economic standards, which results in a wide credibility gap between rhetoric and good intentions on the one hand and reality on the other (Doyal and Gough, 1991, p. 240, Chapter 11 *passim*).

In a globalizing world, then, the way to institutionalize social welfare as an aspect of development would be to express it as a social standard in relation to the economic standard and capacity of nations, e.g. measured by per capita income. Such standards could become something like a social charter for nations albeit adapted to economic capacity. The link with the economic standard would provide an automatic 'social escalator', in that as societies develop economically, their social standard of living rises in tandem. This would make for an upward harmonization in social standards instead of the slide to the bottom that we are witnessing with unregulated globalization today.[5]

We turn next to the question of how these social standards are to be worked out in relation to the economic capacity of nations. Who will formulate these standards and what validity or legitimacy would the latter have? These are important questions and one needs to be able to move from broad principles to the specifics of social protection.[6] We believe that in the last analysis it is social consensus that must indicate appropriate standards. However, other factors, e.g. the experience of other countries and expert opinion, are also relevant. Here the developing countries have an advantage in that they can learn – both positive and negative lessons – from the experience of more developed countries. Moreover the expertise and experience of agencies of the UN, the ILO and the plethora of non-governmental organizations (NGOs) involved with social development constitute a rich resource (Deacon et al., 1997; Doyal and Gough, 1991).

Let us, however, outline a possible approach to formulating the social standards of nations. The WB classifies countries into three broad groups: high, medium and low, in terms of per capita income. The middle income group is further divided into an upper and a lower tier (World Bank, 1997, pp. 206–7). These economic classifications provide a basis for formulating social standards. At the top end of the classification we have rich industrialized countries, most of which already have sizeable welfare states. In such countries universal health care and educational provision, adequate income maintenance programmes to ensure a low to zero level of poverty, universal day care for pre-school children and adequate elder care constitute some of the elements of basic social standards. A basic social standard of this nature would, of course, require welfare 'laggards' such as the US to raise their standards while more advanced welfare states would simply need to maintain their current level of social provision.

At the other end of the scale in the WB's classification we have the very poor countries of Asia and sub-Saharan Africa. At this level of development primary health care, sanitation, safe drinking water, adequate nutrition and the like may constitute basic social standards.[7] Countries at a level of development between these extremes would have commensurate social standards. Although affordability and the feasibility of instituting social programmes would depend on the economic level of nations, there would naturally be some variation around the basic standard, with some countries preferring a higher social standard than the basic. Moreover, aid to economically disadvantaged countries could boost their resources and help them reach or exceed basic standards. At any rate, the aim here is not to work out a neat formula but to arrive at a standard which takes into account expert opinion, public opinion and the level of economic development.

It is important to note that public opinion on state welfare in Western industrial societies both reveals the significance of the social dimension and provides a basis for building social standards. For as we have seen (pp. 57–9) one of the remarkable facts about Western industrialized countries is the continuing popularity of social programmes with strong support for universal programmes such as health care and pensions. These attitudes are common to all Western nations and show remarkable persistence over time (Borre and Scarbrough, 1995; Cook and Barrett, 1992; Taylor-Gooby, 1994). Clearly here is a rock-solid case as well as a benchmark for the formulation of social standards. Indeed, it is no secret that citizens in general and interest groups in particular have been dogged in their defence of existing programmes and standards (Pierson, 1994; Esping-Andersen, 1996c). Some analysts see this as merely a selfish defence of entrenched interests that blocks necessary reform (Esping-Andersen, 1996c, pp. 265–7). There is some truth to this allegation, but to see nothing else in this phenomenon is to miss a vital point.

We would argue that widespread popular support for welfare state institutions and their defence points to something deeper and more fundamental which has not been sufficiently appreciated. It is an attempt on the part of the people to preserve communitarian institutions, i.e. institutions which provide a measure of social security, stability and solidarity and thus sustain a sense of a national community. It is a plea to retain and strengthen the 'social' alongside the economic and political aspects of national life.

But this popular preference for social standards is being set aside by governments on the grounds that the 'social' is unaffordable. Affordability refers to the fact that in a globalized economy, governments must be lean and mean. The competition to become more competitive, in short competitive austerity, means a downward slide in standards of social protection. What seems to be emerging as a result is a double deficit. First, there is a *democratic* deficit in that the popular will is being thwarted as national governments bow to the dictates of a global market place. There is also a loss of democratic control in that what is happening to social standards as a result of global competition is not what national governments, e.g. of the Left, necessarily want. Secondly, there is an emerging *social* deficit which is leading to social degradation and the loss of community. Clearly a principled and supranational defence of social standards is necessary as a complement to the national defence of social programmes. The redefinition of the social and the articulation of basic social standards for nations, sketched in outline above, could be the theoretical underpinning of such a defence. It could be helpful in a number of ways.

First, linking social standards broadly to economic standards could create a level playing field for economic competition and thus leave less scope for social dumping. Secondly, it could provide a 'social escalator', i.e. a built-in mechanism for upward harmonization of social standards. Thirdly, in so far as consensus already exists over social programmes in the population at large in industrialized countries, a social charter for rich countries can perhaps be drawn up without too much difficulty.[8] And if accepted and implemented – or even endorsed with a plan of gradual implementation – it could greatly strengthen the case, as well as the moral argument, for demanding labour rights and other minimum standards (commensurate with the level of economic development) from less developed countries. Finally, the most immediate benefit could be to halt the downward slide of social standards in advanced industrial countries.

One of the issues raised by the idea of basic social standards is that of financing, in short, taxation. In the early 1990s taxes and contributions taken together accounted for just over 38 per cent of GDP (OECD, 1997a, pp. 46–7) and social protection expenditure for around 22 per cent of GDP (OECD, 1994d, pp. 58–61, Tables 1a, 1b, 1c) for the member countries of OECD as a whole. There is no reason why something close to these figures should not be an acceptable level of taxation and expenditure, respectively, in rich countries. Indeed if rich nations are committed to maintaining social standards, then it is likely that they will also converge in their levels of taxation, thus creating tax harmonization and preventing a race to the bottom in taxation. In any case basic social standards leave the question of how the social welfare sector is to be organized and financed entirely open. So long as there is a commitment to maintaining basic standards, each country would be free to devise the means best suited for the purpose. These could, for example, range from direct state provision of benefits and services at one end to private provision mandated by the state at the other.

To sum up: the basic social standards approach would send the message that by all means, let nations, corporations and others compete in the global market place. But let them do so on the basis of an agreed set of social standards. These social standards must not be allowed to become a part of the competitive game but must form a part of the *rules* of the game. In other words if we must globalize, let it be in the form of a *regulated* rather than an *unregulated* globalization.

SUPRANATIONAL ACTION ON SOCIAL POLICY

It is one thing to argue, in principle, the case for basic social standards for nations. It is quite another to be able to demonstrate its feasibility. Clearly the latter belongs to the political economy of transnational social welfare, a large and independent subject in its own right and beyond the scope of this book. Nonetheless it would be remiss on our part not to look, however briefly, at the crucial issue raised by the basic standards approach: namely, given the absence of a global government or regulating authority, what are the prospects of basic social standards becoming a reality? In order to help to answer this question, it might be useful to survey briefly the current approaches and agencies involved – directly or indirectly – in the making of supranational social policy.

Supranational activity concerned with social policy in one form or another can be divided into three broad groupings. First, IGOs driven primarily by a neoliberal economic agenda such as the IMF, the WB and the OECD, exert influence on the economic and social policy of nations. Second, non-economic IGOs, notably the UN and its affiliated agencies, including the ILO, influence policy by way of the promotion of labour and social rights. Their concerns are chiefly humanitarian rather than economistic. Third, regional and other trading agreements among nations provide a forum for addressing social and labour issues transnationally. Prominent among these are the EU, NAFTA and the WTO, which replaced GATT in 1994. Here a mix of economic and human rights considerations are involved. Before we look at these three forms of social policy-making briefly, it might be useful to summarize, in a schematic form, the major actors involved in the globalization process as it relates to social policy (see Figure 7.1).

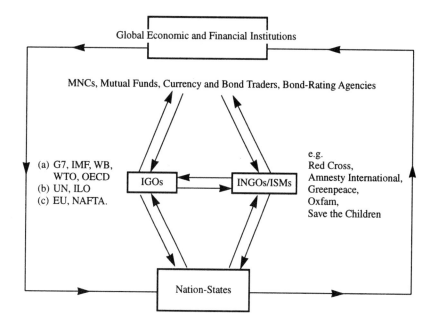

Notes:
(a) Global (economic)
(b) Global (social/humanitarian)
(c) Regional (mixed)
The arrows indicate interaction between major players in the global arena but do not imply either that the intensity of interaction is similar or that power and influence flow equally in both directions. Little is said about the role of INGOs and ISMs in the following pages, not because it is not important but because it is too large a theme to be treated adequately in this book.

Figure 7.1   Global actors and social policy

The Residual Approach to Social Policy

The exercise of economic surveillance and the power to grant loans and arrange financial assistance for developing countries give the IMF and the WB a great deal of influence over the economic and social policies of these countries. The structural adjustment programmes initiated in the 1980s, to which many developing countries have been subjected, are a prime example of this influence (Cornia et al., 1987). More recently, the former communist countries have been faced with similar conditionalities attached to the granting of loans and other economic assistance by these institutions (Deacon et al., 1997, pp. 101, 107). However, in the case of Western industrial nations it is largely by way of policy prescription, expert advice and general economic surveillance that global institutions such as the IMF and OECD influence social policy (see pp. 8–11). Their policy prescriptions which require governments to reduce national debts and deficits mainly through slashing social expenditure and privatizing social welfare amount to the supranational steering of social policy in a neoliberal direction. The same could be said about the insistence that labour markets be made more 'flexible' by, inter alia, weakening the measures of social protection, e.g. unemployment benefits.

Policy advice, the dissemination of research reports and studies, and ministerial conferences form a part of the ideological persuasion involved in such a process. This transnational steering of policy weakens further the autonomy of nation states to chart their own course. By adding to the pressures emanating from financial and capital markets, these global institutions insulate national governments further from the demands of their electorate for social protection.

Yet these IGOs are not directly representative of or accountable to any elected authority. It is no secret that agencies such as the IMF and the WB are largely under the sway of the US, the leading economic power and financial contributor. This is not surprising, given that voting strength in these Bretton Woods institutions is based on the financial status and contribution of member states (Tester, 1992, pp. 137–8). The OECD too represents, by and large, the neoliberal economic orientation associated with the US. True, these agencies differ somewhat in their approach to social policy, e.g. the IMF tends to be the most hard-line neoliberal, the WB is less so, while the OECD shows a greater appreciation of the usefulness of European-style social welfare institutions (Deacon et al., 1997, p. 72, Chapter 3 *passim*). Overall, however, it is fair to say that these IGOs tend to see the institutions of social protection largely as a 'burden' – an impediment to economic development and the free functioning of market forces. Given their economistic approach – focused on deregulation and the extension of the market as the road to prosperity and growth – these IGOs see social policy largely in residual terms, i.e. as an adjunct to economic policies and objectives and one which should provide only a basic social safety net.

Social Policy as Human Rights

The UN and its agencies and affiliates such as the ILO are involved in the formulation of transnational social policy from the standpoint of human rights. While the UN is concerned with the whole gamut of economic and social rights, the ILO focuses on the social protection of workers and the promotion of workers' rights.

The UN's International Covenant on Economic, Social and Cultural Rights (ICESCR), adopted in 1966, includes a comprehensive set of rights such as 'the right to work ... the right to an adequate standard of living ... the right to social security including social insurance ... [and the] right to just and favourable conditions of work', each of which is spelled out in considerable detail (Buergenthal, 1988, pp. 2–3). By the early 1990s over 100 countries had ratified the Covenant (Bilder, 1992, p. 10). Although ratification creates a legal obligation for states to comply, they are expected to implement these rights 'progressively' and 'to the maximum of [their] available resources' (Buergenthal, 1988, p. 44). These caveats turn the Covenant largely into a statement of principles and objectives endorsed by a ratifying country rather than a set of standards to be developed within a specified time-frame.

Significantly, the UN's approach to civil and political rights differs markedly from its approach to economic and social rights. Covenants concerned with the former have no exceptions or caveats. Signatories are expected to implement these rights to the full since they are essentially procedural in nature and do not entail the mobilization of material resources (Buergenthal, 1988, pp. 44–5). Implementation of economic and social rights on the other hand requires the mobilization and redistribution of material resources. Since member states differ widely in respect of economic capacity and other relevant circumstances, compliance with the ICESCR becomes difficult to monitor. Not surprisingly, member states are required to do little more than report on progress from time to time.

Despite its impressive scope, then, the ICESCR remains largely ineffective as an instrument for promoting social rights. First, signing of the Covenant is purely voluntary. Secondly, signing imposes few obligations on nations regarding implementation. Thirdly, while the UN recognizes that the *standards* (as distinct from the *principles*) of social protection which are entailed by economic and social rights cannot be universal and must depend on the level of economic development of a nation, it has not tried to articulate this relationship systematically. This is the problem which we have tried to address through the idea of basic social standards linked to the economic development and capacity of nations.

Among international agencies, the ILO is distinctive in its tripartite composition which represents governments, employers and workers. Membership of

ILO is voluntary, although most countries belong. The ILO is concerned with protecting workers' rights and with improving the conditions of labour, interpreted somewhat widely (Swepston, 1992; Deacon et al., 1997, pp. 73–4). At its annual conferences Recommendations and Conventions are adopted on a wide variety of issues. For example by 1992 the ILO had more than 172 Conventions on its books with 5500 ratifications. It is concerned with such matters as workers' rights to organize, the prohibition of child labour, the health and safety of workplaces and social security, including pensions and medical care (Swepston, 1992, p. 100). Ratification of an ILO Convention by a member state makes it legally binding and members are expected to report regularly on compliance. Although the process is slow and cumbersome, the ILO does monitor the implementation of its Conventions. Through a complaint procedure and a machinery of investigation and reporting, it has achieved some success in securing compliance with ratified Conventions (ibid., pp. 100–108).

However, in common with the ICESCR of the UN, ILO Conventions are universal in form and come up against the fact that member states differ greatly in their level of economic, social and cultural development. The ILO has tried to deal with the problem of diversity through flexibility, e.g. by taking such differences into account in the implementation of the Conventions. For example the Social Security (Minimum Standards) Convention specifies that a ratifying state need adopt only three out of nine types of social security provision contained in it. The Convention also allows temporary exemptions for countries with 'insufficiently developed' economic and other resources (Otting, 1993, pp. 166–7).

Although the ILO does rather better than the UN in securing compliance with its Conventions, it suffers from similar limitations as an agency of international social protection. First, ratification of Conventions is voluntary. Second, although the complaint procedure and the possibility of investigation gives some teeth to ILO Conventions, in the last analysis compliance remains voluntary and thus largely a matter of persuasion. In principle the ILO can recommend sanctions against a recalcitrant member. However, in practice this has never happened. Third, as in the case of the UN's ICESCR, the ILO has recognized the problem of the differing economic capacity of nation states but has not attempted to link labour standards in any systematic way with levels of economic development. Finally, the ILO's remit, unlike that of the UN, is limited to employment-related matters and does not extend to problems of social protection of the population as a whole.

Trading Regimes and Social Policy

Trade Unions in Western countries, notably in the US, have long sought to have a social clause concerned with minimal labour and human rights included in trading agreements with developing countries (Hansson, 1983, pp. 24–8). The principal motivation for the unions' demands for minimum labour rights from these countries has been to limit unfair competition and social dumping and thus to protect industries, jobs and standards in developed countries. This is not to deny that other concerns, notably promoting labour and social rights in developing countries, have also played a part. However the protectionist – and therefore self-serving – aspect of these labour clauses have made them a contentious and divisive issue between the North and South (Deacon et al., 1997, pp. 77–8). The irony of American workers demanding labour and trade union rights for workers in the developing world at the very moment when they themselves are being denied these rights in their own country has not been lost on many commentators (for example Singh, 1988). Moreover critics have drawn attention to the silence of American unions on issues such as the structural adjustment policies of the World Bank and low commodity prices – policies backed by the US – which have had a devastating impact on living standards in many developing countries (ibid., p. 262).

A major limitation of the social clause approach is that it is largely concerned with the basic rights of workers, e.g. the right to organize and to bargain collectively, within the developing world. It has little to say about conditions in industrialized countries. In recent years American workers have succeeded in having a social clause included in some of the trade agreements between the US and developing countries, e.g. the Caribbean Basin Initiative. But the effectiveness of such measures remains unclear since much depends on their implementation and monitoring procedures (see Charnovitz, 1987, pp. 565, 572–4). Attempts to insert a social clause as a part of GATT (now WTO) agreements, and therefore to be applicable more widely, have not been successful so far, chiefly because of the opposition of developing countries.

The Free Trade Agreement signed by the US and Canada and later extended to Mexico through NAFTA provided an opportunity to complement the economic common market in North America with minimum social standards. However, the social dimension was virtually ignored. Later, pressure from labour and other groups opposed to NAFTA resulted in the signing of the North American Agreement on Labour Co-operation, which requires each member country to enforce its own labour laws and other social legislation. These so-called side deals have thus far proven rather ineffective. Moreover they do not create any supranational social or labour standards (Stanford et al., 1993, pp. 56–63). On the other hand NAFTA's deregulatory economic and trading clauses and its notion of a level playing field for competition are heavily weighted against the superior social provision of countries like Canada (see for example, Sanger 1993; Sinclair, 1993). Indeed in Canada the downward harmonization of social provision has already begun. Given the lower levels of economic and social standards in the rest of the Americas, the prospect of a steep decline in Canada's system of social welfare remains very real.

The Social Charter (The Charter of the Fundamental Social Rights of Workers of the European Union) represents the only attempt so far to develop a set of supranational social standards within a regional economic association. The Charter was drawn up by the European Commission in 1989 in preparation for closer economic integration of member countries but also in response to demands for minimum social standards by European trade unions (Silvia, 1991; Rhodes, 1995, p. 96). Opposition on the part of employers and by one of the member states led to the watering down of the original proposals. The Charter, concerned with conditions of work and the social protection of workers is a 'solemn declaration' and not a legally binding instrument. Only some of its provisions, such as those concerned with health and safety and maternity leave (an aspect of gender equity within the work force) have so far been included in binding legislation based on a majority vote rather than unanimous agreement of member states (Ross, 1993, pp. 50–4).

Overall, the status of the Charter as a non-binding document – a declaration of principles and objectives only – came as a great disappointment for European labour and others concerned with social rights (Rhodes, 1995, pp. 96–7). Moreover, one of the principles endorsed by the Maastricht Treaty – a treaty for the monetary union of EU countries – is that of 'subsidiarity', i.e. wherever possible, social and other issues should be dealt with at the local or national rather than the community level. This leaves social policy largely within the scope of the nation state (Ross, 1993, p. 61; Rhodes, 1992, p. 35). On the other hand the principles of solidarity and social citizenship within the European Community have found much less acceptance (Streeck, 1995; Rhodes, 1995, p. 97) (see p. 40). Moreover, globalization is tending to privilege 'flexibility' and deregulation of the labour market in Europe. Compared with NAFTA's meagre concern with labour standards, the European Social Charter looks impressive. In fact it is a relatively modest measure for the protection of workers. The prospect that it might develop into a wider network of social protection does not look very bright (Streeck, 1996; Pierson and Leibfried, 1995).

As we have seen (p. 40), the Maastricht Treaty on European monetary union emphasizes the importance of reducing debt and deficit and controlling inflation. Nations must meet strict targets in respect of these in order to qualify for monetary union. It appears that of the two conflicting tendencies within Europe, namely liberalism and social collectivism, it is the former that is winning out for the moment (Streeck, 1996; Ross, 1995). True, there are other institutions and provisions in place in Europe, e.g. for the protection of human rights and for the reduction of regional economic and social disparity. Together with the Social Chapter of the Maastricht Treaty these amount to a social dimension in the European Union which is by no means insignificant (Deacon et al., 1997, pp. 80–84). It is important to note, however, that unlike NAFTA, the EU is much more than a trading bloc. It has been inspired by the vision of political as well as economic integration. The development of a stronger social dimension within Europe in the future cannot be ruled out although it looks unlikely at the moment.[9]

CONCLUSIONS

Clearly progress toward the development of supranational social standards has been somewhat limited and uneven, more impressive in rhetoric and symbolism than in reality. The influence of the IGOs which have been steering social policy in a residual direction, i.e. towards deregulation and weakening of social protection, has so far been much stronger than that of those seeking to establish social rights. However, the UN, the ILO and the EU, each in its own way has made some progress in formulating, and implementing, labour and social rights across nations. Moreover the UN and its affiliates continue to provide a forum for global discourse on social and humanitarian issues and to help focus attention on problems of poverty, social protection and social justice from a supranational perspective. In recent years special conferences or 'summits' have been held on a variety of issues, e.g. Children (1990), Development (1992), Population (1994), Social Development (1995) and Women (1996). Deliberations and debates on these issues have been followed by proposals for global action.

Despite these and other initiatives discussed earlier, social policy has remained essentially a national concern. The main reasons for limited progress in developing effective transnational social protection are two-fold: first, the absence of global institutions of governance with the authority to formulate binding standards and to ensure their implementation. The second and a related point is that although the important difference between civil and political rights on the one hand and economic and social rights on the other has been recognized, the implications of this difference have not been worked out. As we have argued above, to be viable social rights (or as we have argued, social standards) must be formulated in relation to the level of economic development. Otherwise they are likely to remain abstract principles with little purchase on socio-economic reality.

Although the task of spelling out the link between social standards and economic development is not easy, it is essential for making progress in developing basic social standards applicable globally. However, the first and by far the most difficult problem still remains. In the absence of an international government with democratic authority and accountability, social standards have to rely on voluntary compliance. But voluntarism is likely to be even less effective than in the past because of globalization. The Covenants and Conventions we reviewed above were developed at a time when it was almost conventional wisdom that social standards of nations must rise alongside economic growth. The relation between the two was seen as positive.

We are now in a situation where the economic growth of nations is seen as predicated upon lowering rather than raising social standards. The benign assumptions underlying the long-term, evolutionary perspective of an upward harmonization of standards have little validity today. Social standards in advanced industrial countries are sliding downwards and international action is needed to stop the process.

But what form might it take? And what are its chances of succeeding? The main problem here is that those conditions and social forces which made *national* welfare states possible, e.g. the existence of a state with legitimate authority for rule-making and rule-enforcement, electoral competition and representative government, strong industrial action and protest movements threatening the economic and social stability of nations, nationalism and nation-building imperatives, are unavailable at the international level. Moreover, globalization is disempowering citizens within the nation state as far as social rights are concerned without providing them with any leverage globally. At the same time transnational corporations and the global market place have been empowered hugely through financial deregulation and capital mobility.

In these circumstances prospects for global action on social protection do not look very encouraging. However, in a rudimentary form some of the elements which made the development of social standards possible nationally, are also present at the international level. These could form a nucleus around which further action in support of basic social standards might develop. Let us look at them briefly.

First, movement towards global governance and towards the reform of existing IGOs – including the Bretton Woods institutions – has been slowly gathering momentum (Commission on Global Governance, 1995; Deacon et al., 1997, pp. 89, 205–9). The need to make IGOs more representative, democratic, accountable and efficient is beginning to be recognized. Second, the division of policy-making into economic (Bretton Woods) and non-economic IGOs (UN, ILO) with little co-ordination between the two is acknowledged to be unsatisfactory and in need of reform (Deacon et al., 1997, pp. 207–8). Agencies such as the WB and even the IMF are beginning to acknowledge the importance of the 'social' dimension in development (Deacon et al., 1997, pp. 64, 68–70). Third, and more important, as globalization drives more and more nations into adopting policies of 'competitive austerity', national protest movements against cutbacks and social retrenchment are springing up in many countries. It is not too fanciful to suggest that they might coalesce into an international protest movement in defence of social programmes and standards, for example in OECD countries. Fourth, the 'global civil society' – made up of a wide variety of NGOs, churches and social movements is emerging as a player closely involved with global issues of the environment, development and social justice (ibid., pp. 211–12; Commission on Global Governance, 1995, pp. 253–60). Although somewhat amorphous and lacking in power, global civil society is contributing to a global discourse on social and environmental issues and seems to be growing in influence.

Finally, as Marx, Polanyi and other thinkers have emphasized, sooner or later an unregulated market economy wreaks economic and social havoc. We noted earlier that the unrestricted flow of money around the world has started destabilizing economies and is threatening to plunge the world into a severe recession. Other disequilibria and contradictions of global capitalism, e.g. lack of consumer demand, social unrest, and the weakening of democracy could intensify and compel global regulation. The question is whether we will wait for disaster to strike or forestall such possibilities through appropriate economic and social regulation. The basic belief underlying the argument for international action advanced here is that lessons of history should not be forgotten and that if we deregulate at the national level we could complement that with reregulation at the supranational level. For example a Multinational Agreement on Social Standards (MASS) could parallel the proposed Multinational Agreement on Investment (MAI)[10].

In sum, basic social standards could be an important focal point for regulating the global market economy. Their *raison d'être* would be to preserve the integrity of local and national communities and provide a level playing field for international competition. In this way it might be possible to preserve and/or build that integration between economic and social sectors which is perhaps the most important legacy of the post-WW2 welfare state. At any rate, basic social standards – applicable globally – are of the utmost importance today in that they can provide a degree of stability and continuity for human communities in the context of global economic competition and technological change.

NOTES

1. In 1980, for example, only 0.1 per cent of aged households were poor in Sweden, compared with 9 per cent in West Germany and 18 per cent in UK (Ginsburg, 1992, p. 201, Table A.6).
2. True, much depends on the nature of the country's economy, the degree of international integration and attitudes of capital, the institutional and policy legacy of the golden age.

For example, welfare states in small countries such as Norway, Denmark and Austria show a large measure of continuity and stability.

3. Whether social rights are in a class apart from civil and political rights, and if so with what implications, remains a subject of long-standing debate in the literature of human rights and social policy (Plant et al., 1980). See Mishra (1977, pp. 24–7) for an early statement of the view that social rights are different. In any case, the attempt to operationalize these various rights brings out what is distinctive about social rights. See Doyal and Gough (1991, pp. 230–32).

4. Procedural rights such as freedom of speech and association, and the right to due processes of law do not essentially require the mobilization or distribution of material resources. They rely on procedural action on the part of the state or other agents, e.g. forbearance. Substantive rights such as the right to an adequate income in retirement or the right to medical care on the other hand require the mobilization and/or redistribution of resources.

5. This approach has some similarity with the idea of 'social development' which subsumes economic development but goes beyond it. See Midgley (1997) for an elaboration of social development from the perspective of international social work and welfare.

6. There is a vast literature connected with development studies and the work of international agencies such as United Nations Development Programme, United Nations Research Institute for Social Development, World Health Organization, United Nations Chidren's Fund (UNICEF) relevant to this issue. For a recent attempt to operationalize a universal human needs approach across diverse societies see Doyal and Gough (1991).

7. An example of linking health goals with levels of economic development is provided by World Health Organization. See Doyal and Gough (1991, p. 240).

8. The broad consensus shown by public opinion polls on social welfare in industrialized countries and the established institutions and practices in these countries provide the basis for a realistic statement about basic social standards. While not minimizing the technical and political problems of reaching consensus, it should be possible to make a start with perhaps a few indicators such as maximum permissible poverty rate, and universal access to medical care.

9. For a 'pessimistic' view see Streeck (1995); for a somewhat open-ended, if not cautiously optimistic, view see Pierson and Leibfried (1995).

10. The MAI has been shelved as a result of international mobilization against it and the failure of OECD countries to reach agreement on a number of key issues. Broadly similar objectives are now being pursued through the Transatlantic Economic Partnership (TEP) and the Millennium Round of the WTO.

References

Adnett, N. (1995) 'Social Dumping and European Economic Intervention', *Journal of European Social Policy*, **5**(1).

Albert, M. (1993) *Capitalism against Capitalism*, London, Whurr Publishers.

Andrews, G. (ed.) (1991) *Citizenship*, London, Lawrence and Wishart.

Appelbaum, E. (1992) 'Structural Change and the Growth of Part-Time and Temporary Employment' in du Rivage, V.L. (ed.) *New Policies for the Part-Time and Contingent Work Force*, Armonk, M.E. Sharpe.

Baines, C. et al. (1991) *Women's Caring*, Toronto, McClelland and Stewart.

Baker, M. (1997) 'Parental Benefit Policies and the Gendered Division of Labour', *Social Service Review,* March.

Balls, E. (1994) 'No More Jobs for the Boys' in Michie, J. and Grieve Smith, J. (eds) *Unemployment in Europe*, London, Academic Press.

Barbalet, J.M. (1988) *Citizenship*, Milton Keynes, Open University Press.

Barlow, M. and Campbell, B. (1995) *Straight Through the Heart*, Toronto, HarperCollins.

Barnet, R.J. and Kavanagh, J. (1994) *Global Dreams*, New York, Simon and Schuster.

Barry, B. (1990) *Welfare*, Milton Keynes, Open University Press.

Bashevkin, S. (1994) 'Confronting Neo-Conservatism: Anglo-American Women's Movements under Thatcher, Reagan and Mulroney', *International Political Science Review*, **15**(3).

Battle, K. (1997) *Transformation: Canadian Social Policy Since 1985* (Mimeo), Ottawa, Caledon Institute of Social Policy.

Belous, R. (1989) *The Contingent Economy*, Washington, DC, National Planning Association.

Bensaid, D. (1996) 'Class Struggles in France', *New Left Review*, **215**.

Bienenfeld, M. (1994) 'Capitalism and the Nation State in the Dog Days of the Twentieth Century', in Miliband, R. and Panitch, L. (eds) *The Socialist Register 1994*, London, Merlin.

Bilder, B. (1992) 'Overview of International Human Rights Law', in Hannum, H. (ed.) *Guide to International Human Rights*, 2nd edn, Philadelphia, University of Philadelphia Press.

Binstock, R.H. (1992) 'Older Voters and the 1992 Presidential Election', *The Gerontologist*, **32**(5).

Borre, O. and Scarborough, E. (eds.) (1995) *The Scope of Government*, New York, Oxford University Press.

Boston, J. (1993) 'Reshaping Social Policy in New Zealand', *Fiscal Studies*, **14**(3).

Bowd, G. (1995) 'France: la Fracture Sociale', *New Left Review*, **212**.

Bowley, G. and Studemann, F. (1997) 'Job evaluation needed', *Financial Times*, 18 November.

Boyer, R. and Drache, D. (eds) (1996) *States Against Markets*, London and New York, Routledge.

Brecher, J. and Costello, T. (1994) *Global Village or Global Pillage?* Boston, MA, South End Press.

Brodie, J. (1995) *Politics on the Margins: Restructuring the Canadian Women's Movement*, Halifax, Fernwood Publishing.

Bruce, M. (1965) *The Coming of the Welfare State*, London, Batsford.

Brummer, A. and Watts, J. (1998) 'Dark shadow falls over the sun nation', *Guardian Weekly*, 14 June.

Buergenthal, T. (1988) *International Human Rights in a Nutshell*, St Paul, MN, West Publishing.

Burghes, L. (1990) 'Workfare: Lessons from the US Experience', in Manning N. and Ungersen C. (eds) *Social Policy Review 1989–90*, Harlow, Essex, Longman.

Cameron, D. and Finn, E. (1996) *10 Deficit Myths*, Ottawa, Canadian Centre for Policy Alternatives.

Canadian Dimension (1997) 'Editorial', *Canadian Dimension*, Jan.–Feb.

Castells, M. (1998) *End of Millennium Vol. III*, Oxford and Malden, MA, Blackwell.

Castles, F.G. (1996) 'Needs-based Strategies of Social Protection in Australia and New Zealand', in Esping-Andersen, G. (ed.) *Welfare States in Transition*, London, Sage.

Castles, F.G. (ed.) (1982) *The Impact of Parties*, London, Sage.

Castles, F.G. and Pierson, C. (1996) 'A New Convergence? Recent policy developments in the United Kingdon, Australia and New Zealand', *Policy and Politics*, **24**(3).

CCPA (Canadian Centre for Policy Alternatives) (1996) 'IMF calls for global public spending cuts', *CCPA Monitor*, **3**(3).

CCPA (Canadian Centre for Policy Alternatives) (1997) 'TNEs almost tax-free in Australia, too' *CCPA Monitor*, **3**(8), February.

CEC (Commission of the European Communities) (1993) 'Growth, Competitiveness, Employment: The Challenges and Ways Forward into the 21st Century', *Bulletin of the European Communities*, Supplement 6/93, Luxembourg.

Charnovitz, S. (1987) 'The Influence of International Labour Standards on the World Trading Regime: a Historical Overview', *International Labour Review*, **126**(5).

Chorney, H. (1996) 'Debts, Deficits and Full Employment', in Boyer, R. and Drache, D. (eds) *States Against Markets*, London and New York, Routledge.

Clarke, T. and Barlow, M. (1997) *MAI: Multilateral Agreement on Investment and the Threat to Canadian Sovereignty*, Toronto, Stoddart.

Clasen, J. and Gould, A. (1995) 'Stability and Change in Welfare States: Germany and Sweden in the 1990's', *Policy and Politics*, **23**(3).

Cloud, S.W. (1992) 'The Lessons of Perot', *Time*, 16 November.

Collier, K. (1995) 'Global Finance Against State Intervention', *Socialist Studies Bulletin*, **42**.

Commission on Global Governance (1995) *Our Global Neighbourhood*, Oxford, Oxford University Press.

Confalonieri, M.A. and Newton, K. (1995) 'Taxing and Spending: Tax Revolt or Tax Protest?' in Borre, O. and Scarbrough, E. (eds) *The Scope of Government*, Oxford, Oxford University Press.

Cook, F.L. and Barrett, E.J. (1992) *Support for the American Welfare State*, New York, Columbia University Press.

Cornia, G.A. et al. (1987) *Adjustment with a Human Face*, 2 vols, Oxford, Clarendon Press.

CSJ (Commission on Social Justice) (1994) *Social Justice: Strategies for National Renewal*, London, Vintage Books.

Czerny, P.G. (1997) 'Paradoxes of the Competition State: The Dynamics of Political Globalization', *Government and Opposition*, **32**(2).

Day, C.L. (1990) *What Older Americans Think*, Princeton, NJ, Princeton University Press.

Deacon, B. et al. (1997) *Global Social Policy*, London, Sage.

Dicken, P. (1992) *Global Shift*, London, Paul Chapman Publishing.

Dillon, J. (1997) *Turning the Tide: Confronting the Money Traders*, Ottawa, Canadian Centre for Policy Alternatives.

Dominelli, L. (1991) *Women Across Continents*, New York, Harvester Wheatsheaf.

Doyal, L. and Gough, I. (1991) *A Theory of Human Need*, London, Macmillan.

Drohan, M. (1994) 'Global economy foils the taxman', *Globe and Mail*, 4 April.

du Rivage, V.L. (1992) 'New Policies for the Part-Time and Contingent Work Force', in du Rivage, V.L. (ed.) *New Policies for the Part-Time and Contingent Work Force*, Armonk, M.E. Sharpe.

Elliott, L. (1996) 'Blair takes a right-hand turn to No. 10', *Guardian Weekly*, 14 April.

Elliott, L. (1997) 'Flexible Labour Policy No Aid to Jobs – OECD', *Guardian Weekly*, 13 July, p. 7.

Elliott, L. (1998) 'Capitalism on a fast road to ruin', *Guardian Weekly*, 13 July.

Espada, J.C. (1996) *Social Citizenship Rights: A Critique of F.A. Hayek and Raymond Plant*, London, Macmillan.

Esping-Andersen, G. (1985) *Politics Against Markets*, Princeton, NJ, Princeton University Press.

Esping-Andersen, G. (1990) *The Three Worlds of Welfare Capitalism*, Princeton, NJ, Princeton University Press.

Esping-Andersen, G. (1996a) 'After the Golden Age? Welfare State Dilemmas in a Global Economy', in Esping-Andersen, G. (ed.) *Welfare States in Transition*, London, Sage.

Esping-Andersen, G. (1996b) Welfare States without Work: the Impasse of Labour Shedding and Familialism in Continental European Social Policy', in Esping-Andersen, G. (ed.) *Welfare States in Transition*, London, Sage.

Esping-Andersen, G. (1996c) 'Positive-Sum Solutions in a World of Trade-offs?' in Esping-Andersen, G. (ed.) *Welfare States in Transition*, London, Sage.

European Parliament (1992) 'Maastricht: the Treaty on European Union', *European Parliament*, Part II, Luxembourg, Office for Official Publications of the European Communities.

Evans, P. and Wekerle, G. (eds) (1997) *Women and the Canadian Welfare State*, Toronto, University of Toronto Press.

Field, F. (1995) 'The poison in the welfare state', *Daily Telegraph*, 14 May.

Financial Post (1998) 'Paul Martin's quest for a new world order', *Financial Post*, 28 October, C5.

Fukuyama, F. (1992) *The End of History and the Last Man*, New York, Free Press.

Fulcher, J. (1994) 'The Social-Democratic Model in Sweden: Termination or Restoration?' *The Political Quarterly*, **65**(2).

Garrett, G. (1998) *Partisan Politics in the Global Economy*, Cambridge, Cambridge University Press.

Gee, M. (1998) 'The Real End of Japan Inc', *Globe and Mail*, 18 April.

Gelb, J. (1989) *Feminism and Politics: A Comparative Perspective*, Berkeley, University of California Press.

Gelb, J. (1990) 'Feminism and Political Action', in Dalton, R.J. and Kuechler, M. (eds) *Challenging the Political Order: New Social and Political Movements in Western Democracies*, New York, Oxford University Press.

George, V. (1996) 'The Future of the Welfare State', in George, V. and Taylor-Gooby, P. (eds) *European Welfare Policy*, London, Macmillan.

George, V. (1998) 'Political Ideology, Globalisation and Welfare Futures in Europe', *Journal of Social Policy*, **27**(1).

George, V. and Miller, S. (eds) (1994) *Social Policy Towards 2000*, London, Routledge.

George, V. and Wilding, P. (1994) *Welfare and Ideology*, Hemel Hempstead, Harvester Wheatsheaf.

Ghai, D. (1991) *The IMF and the South: Social Impact of Crisis and Adjustment*, London, Zed Books.

Gifford, C.G. (1990) *Canada's Fighting Seniors*, Toronto, James Lorimer and Co.

Ginn, J. (1996) 'Grey Power: Age-based Organisations' Response to Structural Inequalities', in D. Taylor (ed.) *Critical Social Policy: A Reader*, London, Sage.

Ginsburg, N. (1992) *Divisions of Welfare*, London, Sage.

Glasman, M. (1997) The Seige of the German Social Market', *New Left Review*, **225**.

Globe and Mail (1997) 'EU develops plan to cut joblessness', *Globe and Mail*, 22 November.

Gold, H.J. (1995) 'Third Party Voting in Presidential Elections', *Political Research Quarterly*, **48**(4).

Goodhart, D. (1993) 'Social Dumping: Hardly an Open and Shut Case', *Financial Times*, 4 February.

Goodman, R. and Peng, I. (1996) 'The East Asian Welfare States', in Esping-Andersen, G. (ed.) *Welfare States in Transition*, London, Sage.

Gotting, U. et al. (1994) 'The Long Road to Long-term Care Insurance in Germany', *Journal of Public Policy*, **14**(3).

Gould, A. (1993) *Capitalist Welfare Systems*, London, Longman.

Gould, A. (1996) 'Sweden: The Last Bastion of Social Democracy', in George, V. and Taylor-Gooby, P. (eds) *European Welfare Policy*, London, Macmillan.

Gray, G. (1990) 'Social Policy by Stealth', *Policy Options*, **11**(2).

Greider, W. (1993) *Who Will Tell the People*? New York, Touchstone/Simon and Schuster.

Greider, W. (1998) *One World, Ready or Not*, New York, Touchstone/Simon and Schuster.

Grinspun, R. and Cameron, M.A. (eds) (1993) *The Political Economy of North American Free Trade*, Montreal and Kingston, McGill-Queen's University Press.

Guardian Weekly (1995) 'France takes to the streets', *Guardian Weekly*, 10 December.

Habermas, J. (1976) *Legitimation Crisis*, London, Heinemann.

Hall, P. A. (1987) 'The Evolution of Economic Policy under Mitterand', in Ross, G. et al. (eds) *The Mitterand Experiment*, Cambridge, Polity.

Hansson, G. (1983) *Social Clauses and International Trade*, Beckenham, Croom Helm.

Harding, P. (1998) 'Models of Social Welfare and Gender Equality: US, USSR and Sweden' (unpublished PhD dissertation). University of Toronto, Faculty of Social Work.

Held, D. (1995) *Democracy and the Global Order*, Cambridge, Polity.

Helleiner, E (1996) 'Post-Globalization: Is the Financial Liberalization Trend Likely to be Reversed?' in Boyer, R. and Drache, D. (eds) *States Against Markets*, London and New York, Routledge.

Heller, H. (1996) 'Gulliver's Troubles or Lilliput Fights Back', *Canadian Dimension*, May–June.

Hicks, A. et al. (1995) 'The Programmatic Emergence of the Social Security State', *American Sociological Review*, **60**(3).

Hills, J. (ed.) (1995) *New Inequalities: The Changing Distribution of Income and Wealth in the United Kingdom*, Cambridge, Cambridge University Press.

Hirst, P. and Thompson, G. (1996) *Globalization in Question*, Cambridge, Polity.

Hooyman, N. and Gonyea, J. (1995) *Feminist Perspectives on Family Care: Policies for Gender Justice*, Thousand Oaks, CA, Sage.

Horsman, M. and Marshall, A. (1995) *After the Nation-State*, London, Harper-Collins.

Hort, S.E.O. and Kuhnle, S. (1998) 'Recent Changes in Emerging East and South-east Asian Welfare States – Is there Social Dumping?' Paper presented at XIVth World Congress of Sociology, Montreal.

Huber, E. and Stephens, J.D. (1998) 'Internationalization and the Social Democratic Model', *Comparative Political Studies*, **31**(3).

Huseby, B.M. (1995) 'Attitudes towards the Size of Government', in Borre, O. and Scarbrough E. (eds) *The Scope of Government*, Oxford, Oxford University Press.

Hutton, W. (1995a) *The State We're In*, London, Jonathan Cape.

Hutton, W. (1995b) 'High-risk strategy is not paying off', *Guardian Weekly*, 2 November.

ILO (International Labour Organization) (1995) *World Employment 1995*, Geneva, ILO.

IMF (1994) *World Economic Outlook*, May, Washington, DC.

IMF (1997) *World Economic Outlook*, May, Washington, DC.

Johnson, N. (1990) *Reconstructing the Welfare State*, Hemel Hempstead, Harvester Wheatsheaf.

Jones, C. (1993) 'The Pacific Challenge: Confucian Welfare States' in Jones, C. (ed.) *New Perspectives on the Welfare State in Europe*, London, Routledge.

Kahne, H. (1994) 'Part-time work: a reassessment for a changing economy', *Social Service Review*, **68**(3).

Kamerman, S. (1996) 'The New Politics of Child and Family Policies', *Social Work*, September, **41**(5).

Katzenstein, M.F. and Mueller, C.M. (eds) (1987) *The Women's Movement of the United States and Western Europe*, Philadelphia, Temple University Press.

Kelly, R. (1995) 'Derivatives: A Growing Threat to the International Financial System', in Michie, J. and Smith, J.G. (eds) *Managing the Global Economy*, Oxford, Oxford University Press.

Kelsey, J. (1995) *Economic Fundamentalism*, London, Pluto.

Kester, W.C. (1996) 'American and Japanese Corporate Governance', in Berger, S. and Dore, R. (eds) *National Diversity and Global Capitalism*, Ithaca and London, Cornell University Press.

King, D.S. (1987) *The New Right*, London, Macmillan.

Korpi, W. (1983) *The Democratic Class Struggle*, London, Routledge.

Korten, D.C. (1995) *When Corporations Rule the World*, West Hartford, CT and San Francisco, CA, Kumarian Press and Berrett-Koehler Publishers.

Kosonen, P. (1998) 'The Impact of Globalization and Global Actors on Small Welfare States'. Paper presented at XIVth World Congress of Sociology, Montreal.

Kurzer, P. (1991) 'The Internationalisation of Business and Domestic Class Compromises: A Four Country Study', *West European Politics*, **14**(4).

Larkin, J. and O'Neill, E. (eds) (1998) *Confronting the Cuts: A Sourcebook for Women in Ontario*, North York, Inanna Publications.

Lee, H. K. (1987) 'The Japanese Welfare State in Transition', in Friedman, R. R. et al. (eds) *Modern Welfare States*, New York, New York University Press.

Leibfried, S. and Pierson, P. (1994) 'The Prospects for Social Europe', in Swann, A. (ed.) *Social Policy Beyond Borders*, Amsterdam, Amsterdam University Press.

Leibfried, S. and Pierson, P. (1995a) 'Semisovereign Welfare States: Social Policy in a Multitiered Europe', in Leibfried, S. and Pierson, P. (eds) *European Social Policy*, Washington, DC, The Brookings Institution.

Leibfried, S. and Pierson, P. (eds) (1995b) *European Social Policy*, Washington, DC, The Brookings Institution.

Ley, R. and Poret, P. (1997) 'The New OECD Members and Liberalisation', *The OECD Observer*, **205**.

Marshall, T.H. (1950) *Citizenship and Social Class and other Essays*, Cambridge, Cambridge University Press.

Martin, A. (1994) 'Labour, the Keynesian Welfare State, and the Changing International Political Economy', in Stubbs, R. and Underhill, G.R.D. (eds) *Political Economy and the Changing Global Order*, New York, St Martin's Press.

Martin, H.P. and Schumann, H. (1997) *The Global Trap*, London, Zed Books.

Maruo, N. (1986) 'The Development of the Welfare Mix in Japan' in Rose, R. and Shiratori, R. (eds) *The Welfare State East and West*, New York, Oxford University Press.

Massey, P. (1995) *New Zealand: Market Liberalization in a Developed Economy*, New York, St Martin's Press.

McBride, S. and Shields, J. (1997) *Dismantling a Nation*, Halifax, Fernwood Publishing.

McBride Stetson, D. (1990) *Women's Rights in the U.S.A.: Policy Debates and Gender Roles*, Pacific Grove, Brooks/Cole.

McCarthy, S. (1997) 'Ottawa to fight expatriation of profits', *Globe and Mail*, 12 September.

McDonald, L. (1995) 'Editorial: Retirement for the Rich and Retirement for the Poor', *Canadian Journal on Aging*, **14**(3).

McLaughlin, E. (1994) 'Flexibility or polarization?' in White, M. (ed.) *Unemployment and Public Policy in a Changing Labour Market*, London, Policy Studies Institute.

McQuaig, L. (1998) *The Cult of Impotence*, Toronto, Viking Penguin.

Midgley, J. (1997) *Social Welfare in Global Context*, Thousand Oaks, CA, Sage.

Milner, M. and Tran, M. (1995) 'Europe and US feel the pinch', *Guardian Weekly*, 10 September.

Mishel, L. and Bernstein, J. (1994) *The State of Working America 1994–95*, Armonk, M.E. Sharpe.

Mishel, L. et al. (1997) *The State of Working America 1996–97*, Armonk, M.E. Sharpe.

Mishra, R. (1977) *Society and Social Policy*, London, Macmillan.

Mishra, R. (1984) *The Welfare State in Crisis*, Brighton, Wheatsheaf Books.

Mishra, R. (1990) *The Welfare State in Capitalist Society*, Hemel Hempstead, Harvester Wheatsheaf.

Mishra, R. (1996) 'The Welfare of Nations', in Boyer, R. and Drache, D. (eds) *States Against Markets*, London and New York, Routledge.

Moody, K. (1987) 'Reagan, the Business Agenda and the Collapse of Labour', in Miliband, R. et al. (eds) *Socialist Register 1987*, London, Merlin Press.

Morley, M. and Petras, J. (1998) 'Wealth and Poverty in the National Economy', in Lo, C.Y.H. and Schwartz, M. (eds) *Social Policy and the Conservative Agenda*, Malden, MA, Blackwell.

Motohashi, R. and Nezu, R. (1997) 'Why do Countries Perform Differently?' *The OECD Observer*, **206**.

Mulgan, R. (1995) 'The Democratic Failure of Single-Party Government:

The New Zealand Experience', *Australian Journal of Political Science*, **30** (Special Issue).

Muller, W.C. (1994) 'Political Traditions and the Role of the State', *West European Politics*, **17**(3).

Myles, J. (1996) 'When Markets Fail: Social Welfare in Canada and the United States', in Esping-Andersen, G. (ed.) *Welfare States in Transition*, London, Sage.

Neyer, J. and Seeleib-Kaiser, M. (1995) *Bringing the Economy Back In: Economic Globalization and the Re-Commodification of the Workforce*, Bremen, Centre for Social Policy Research.

Nickell, S. (1997) 'Unemployment and Labor Market Rigidities: Europe Versus North America', *Journal of Economic Perspectives*, **11**(3).

Nolan, B. (1994) 'Labour market institutions, industrial restructuring and unemployment in Europe', in Michie, J. and Grieve Smith, J. (eds) *Unemployment in Europe*, London, Academic Press.

Norman, P. (1997) 'Calm Cloaks a Sense of Unease', *Financial Times* (Survey: Germany), 18 November.

O'Connor, J. (1996) 'From Women in the Welfare State to Gendering Welfare State Regimes', *Current Sociology*, **44**(2), Summer.

O'Connor, J. (1973) *The Fiscal Crisis of the State*, New York, St Martin's Press.

O'Connor, K. (1996) *Neutral Ground? Abortion Politics in an Age of Absolutes*, Boulder, Westview Press.

OECD (1985) *Social Expenditure 1960–1990*, Paris.

OECD (1988) *Economic Outlook: Historical Statistics 1960–1986*, Paris.

OECD (1994a) *The OECD Jobs Study: Facts, Analysis, Strategies*, Paris.

OECD (1994b) *The OECD Jobs Study: Evidence and Explanations Part I – Labour Market Trends and Underlying Forces of Change*, Paris.

OECD (1994c) *The OECD Jobs Study: Evidence and Explanations Part II – The Adjustment Potential of the Labour Market*, Paris.

OECD (1994d) *Social Policy Studies No. 2: New Orientations for Social Policy*, Paris.

OECD (1994e) *Economic Surveys: Germany*, Paris.

OECD (1995a) *Introduction to the OECD Codes of Liberalisation*, Paris.

OECD (1995b) *The OECD Jobs Study: Implementing the Strategy*, Paris.

OECD (1995c) *Economic Surveys: Japan*, Paris.

OECD (1995d) *Historical Statistics 1960–1993*, Paris.

OECD (1996a) *Economic Surveys: New Zealand*, Paris.

OECD (1996b) *Economic Surveys: United States*, Paris.

OECD (1997a) 'OECD in Figures' (Supplement to *The OECD Observer*, **206**).

OECD (1997b) *Economic Surveys: Australia*, Paris.

OECD (1997c) *Economic Surveys: United States*, Paris.

OECD (1997d) *Employment Outlook*, Paris.

OECD (1997e) *Economic Surveys: Germany*, Paris.

OECD (1997f) 'The OECD Employment Outlook: Low Wage Jobs: Stepping Stones or Traps?' *The OECD Observer*, **208**, October/November.

OECD (1998) *Economic Outlook*, **63**, June, Paris.

Ohmae, K. (1990) *The Borderless World*, New York, Collins.

Okamoto, T. (1998) 'Home Help Services in Japan'. Paper presented at Symposium on 'Ageing Society and the Welfare State', Vedback, Denmark.

Olsen, G.M. (1996) 'Re-modeling Sweden: The Rise and Demise of the Compromise in a Global Economy', *Social Problems*, **43**(1).

Olsson, S.E. and McMurphy, S. (1993) 'Social Policy in Sweden: The Swedish Model in Transition', *Social Policy Review 5*, Canterbury, Social Policy Association.

Orr, A. (1995) 'New Zealand: The Results of Openness', *The OECD Observer*, **192**.

Osberg, L. and Fortin, P. (1996) *Unnecessary Debts*, Toronto, James Lorimer.

Osberg, L. et al. (1995) *Vanishing Jobs*, Toronto, Lorimer.

Otting, A. (1993) 'International labour standards: a framework for social security', *International Labour Review*, **132**(2).

Owens, J. (1993) 'Globalisation: The Implications for Tax Policies', *Fiscal Studies*, **14**(3).

Peele, G. (1996) 'Social Policy and the Clinton Presidency', in May, M. et al. (eds) *Social Policy Review 8*, London, Social Policy Assocation.

Pekkarinen, J. et al. (1992) *Social Corporatism: A Superior Economic System*? New York, Oxford University Press.

Pempel, T.J. (1989) 'Japan's Creative Conservatism', in Castles, F.G. (ed.) *The Comparative History of Public Policy*, New York, Oxford University Press.

Peng, I. (1999 forthcoming) 'The Japanese Welfare State: Perspectives and Patterns of Change', *Social Policy and Administration*.

Petrella, R. (1996) 'Globalization and Internationalization', in Boyer, R. and Drache, D. (eds) *States Against Markets*, London and New York, Routledge.

Pierson, P. (1994) *Dismantling the Welfare State?* Cambridge, Cambridge University Press.

Pierson, P. and Leibfried, S. (1995) 'The Dynamics of Social Policy Integration', in Leibfried, S. and Pierson, P. (eds) *European Social Policy*, Washington DC, The Brookings Institution.

Piven, F.F. (1995) 'Is it Global Economics or Neo-Laissez-faire?' *New Left Review*, **213**.

Plant, R., Lesser, H., and Taylor-Gooby, P. (1980) *Political Philosophy and Social Welfare*, London, Routledge.

Pontusson, J. (1992) 'At the End of the Third Road: Swedish Social Democracy in Crisis', *Politics and Society*, **20** (3).

Reich, R.B. (1992) *The Work of Nations*, New York, Vintage Books.

Rhodes, M. (1992) 'The Future of the "social dimension": labour market regulations in post-1992 Europe', *Journal of Common Market Studies*, **30**(1).

Rhodes, M. (1995) 'A regulatory conundrum: industrial relations and the social dimension' in Leibfried, S. and Pierson, P. (eds) *European Social Policy*, Washington DC, The Brookings Institution.

Rhodes, M. (1996) 'Globalisation and West European Welfare States: A Critical Review of Recent Debates', *Journal of European Social Policy*, **6**(4).

Rieger, E. and Leibfried, S. (1998) 'Welfare State Limits to Globalization', *Politics and Society*, **26**(3).

Rifkin, J. (1995) *The End of Work*, New York, G.P. Putnam's Sons.

Roche, M. (1992) *Rethinking Citizenship*, Cambridge, Polity.

Ross, G. (1993) 'Social Policy in the New Europe', *Studies in Political Economy*, **40**.

Ross, G. (1995) 'Assessing the Delors Era and Social Policy' in Leibfried, S. and Pierson, P. (eds.) *European Social Policy*, Washington, DC, The Brookings Institution.

Ruggie, M. (1984) *State and Working Women: A Comparative Study of Britain and Sweden*, Princeton, NJ, Princeton University Press.

Ryan, B. (1992) *Feminism and the Women's Movement*, New York and London, Routledge.

Sainsbury, D. (1994) (ed.) *Gendering Welfare States*, London, Sage.

Sainsbury, D. (1996) *Gender, Equality and Welfare States*, Cambridge, Cambridge University Press.

Sandford, C. (1993) *Successful Tax Reform*, Perrymead, Bath, Fiscal Publications.

Sanger, M. (1993) 'Public Services' in Cameron, D. and Watkins, M. (eds) *Canada Under Free Trade*, Toronto, James Lorimer.

Sassoon, A.S. (ed.) (1987) *Women and the State*, London, Hutchinson.

Sassoon, D. (1996) *One Hundred Years of Socialism*, New York, The New Press.

Schaeffer, R.K. (1997) *Understanding Globalization*, Lanham, MD, Rowman and Littlefield Publishers.

Schregle, J. (1993) 'Dismissal Protection in Japan', *International Labour Review*, **132**(4).

Silvia, S.J. (1991) 'The Social Charter of the European Community: A Defeat for European Labour', *Industrial and Labour Relations Review*, **44**(4).

Sinclair, S. (1993) 'Provincial Powers' in Cameron, D. and Watkins, M. (eds) *Canada Under Free Trade*, Toronto, James Lorimer.

Sinfield, A. (1994) 'The Latest Trends in Social Security in the United Kingdom', in Ploug, N. and Kvist, J. (eds) *Recent Trends in Cash Benefits in Europe*, Copenhagen, Danish National Institute of Social Research.

Singh, A. (1988) 'Southern Competition, Labour Standards and Industrial Development in the North and South' in Herzenberg, S. and Perez-Lopez, J.F. (eds.) *Labour Standards and Development in the Global Economy*, Washington, DC, US Department of Labor, Bureau of International Affairs.

Stanford, J. et al. (1993) *Social Dumping under North American Free Trade*, Ottawa, Centre for Policy Alternatives.

Steinmo, S. (1994) 'The End of Redistribution? International Pressures and Domestic Tax Policy Choices', *Challenge*, **37**(6).

Stephens, J.D. (1979) *The Transition from Capitalism to Socialism*, Urbana and Chicago, University of Illinois Press.

Stephens, J.D. (1996) 'The Scandinavian Welfare States', in Esping-Andersen, G. (ed.) *Welfare States in Transition*, London, Sage.

Stephens, R. (1993) 'Radical Tax Reform in New Zealand', *Fiscal Studies*, **14**(3).

Streeck, W. (1993) 'The Social Dimension of the European Economy', in Mayes, D. et al. *Public Interest and Market Pressure*, London, Macmillan.

Streeck, W. (1995) 'From Market Making to State Building? Reflections on the Political Economy of European Social Policy', in Leibfried, S. and Pierson, P. (eds) *European Social Policy*, Washington, DC, The Brookings Institution.

Streeck, W. (1996) 'Public Power Beyond the Nation-State' in Boyer, R. and Drache, D. (eds) *States against Markets*, London, Routledge.

Sullivan, K, (1997) 'Costs of Economic Equality Questioned', *Guardian Weekly*, 8 June.

Swardson, A. (1996) 'Canada's Slimline Economy', *Guardian Weekly*, 14 July.

Swepston, L. (1992) 'Human Rights Complaint Procedures of the International Labour Organization' in Hannum, H. (ed.) *Guide to International Human Rights*, 2nd edn, Philadelphia, University of Philadelphia Press.

Taylor-Gooby, P. (1994) 'Taxing Time', *New Statesman and Society*, 2 December.

Taylor-Gooby, P. (1996a) 'The United Kingdom: Radical Departures and Political Consensus', in George, V. and Taylor-Gooby, P. (eds) *European Welfare Policy*, London, Macmillan.

Taylor-Gooby, P. (1996b) 'The Response of Government: Fragile Convergence?' in George, V. and Taylor-Gooby, P. (eds) *European Welfare Policy*, London, Macmillan.

Teeple, G. (1995) *Globalization and the Decline of Social Reform*, Toronto, Garamond Press.

Temple, P. (1995) 'Changing the Rules in New Zealand: The Electoral Reform Agenda of 1992 and 1993', *The Political Quarterly*, **66**(2).

Tester, F.J. (1992) 'The Disenchanted Democracy: Canada in the Global Economy of the 1990's', *Canadian Review of Social Policy*, **29**(30).

The Economist (1995) 'The Changing Face of the Welfare State', 26 August.

The Economist (1996a) 'American Survey', 11 November.

The Economist (1996b) 'Germany: Is the model broken?', 4 May.

Therborn, G. (1984) 'The Prospects of Labour and the Transformation of Advanced Capitalism', *New Left Review*, **145**.

Therborn, G. (1986) *Why Some Peoples Are More Unemployed Than Others*, London, Verso.

Thompson, N. (1996) 'Supply-side Socialism: The Political Economy of New Labour', *New Left Review*, **216**.

Thurow, L.C. (1996) *The Future of Capitalism*, New York, William Morrow and Co.

Timmins, N. (1994) 'Massive public support for the welfare state', *The Independent*, 17 November.

Toinet, M.-F. (1996) 'Emplois "Flexibles" Société en Miettes', *Manière de Voir*, **31** (Le Nouveau Modèle Amèricain).

Traynor, I. (1996) 'Unions fight Kohl's cuts', *Guardian Weekly*, 23 June.

Turner, B.S. (1986) *Citizenship and Capitalism*, London, Allen and Unwin.

ul Haq, M. et al. (1996) *The Tobin Tax*, Oxford, Oxford University Press

UN (United Nations) (1994) *World Investment Report 1994*, New York and Geneva.

UN (United Nations) (1995) *World Investment Report 1995*, New York and Geneva.

Vinocur, J. (1997) 'Subtlety of German Wealth Masks Inequalities', *Globe and Mail*, 18 October.

Wad, P. (1998) 'Welfare Implications of the Financial Crisis in East and Southeast Asia'. Paper presented at Symposium on 'Ageing Society and the Welfare State', Vedbaek, Denmark.

Wade, R. (1996) 'Globalization and Its Limits', in Berger, S. and Dore, R. (eds) *National Diversity and Global Capitalism*, Ithaca and London, Cornell University Press.

Walker, M. (1998) 'Eleven head for monetary union', *Guardian Weekly*, 8 March.

Watanuki, J. (1986). 'Is there "Japanese-type Welfare Society"?' *International Sociology*, **1**(3).

Waters, M. (1995) *Globalization*, London, Routledge.

Webster, P. and Steele, J. (1997) 'Now France takes dramatic left turn', *Guardian Weekly*, 8 June.

Weir, A. and Wilson, E. (1984) 'The British Women's Movement', *New Left Review*, **148**.

Weiss, L. (1997) 'Globalization and the Myth of the Powerless State', *New Left Review*, **225**.

Weiss, L. (1998) *The Myth of the Powerless State*, Ithaca, Cornell University Press.

Wilensky, H.L. and Lebeaux, C.N. (1965) *Industrial Society and Social Welfare*, 2nd edn, New York, The Free Press.

Wilks, S. (1996) 'Class Compromise and the International Economy: The Rise and Fall of Swedish Social Democracy', *Capital and Class*, **58**.

Williams, F. (1989) *Social Policy: A Critical Introduction*, Cambridge, Polity.

Williams, F. (1992) 'Somewhere Over the Rainbow: Universality and Diversity in Social Policy', in Manning, N. and Pape, R. (eds) *Social Policy Review 4*, London, Social Policy Association.

Wilson, E. (1977) *Women and the Welfare State*, London, Tavistock.

Woolcock, S. (1996) 'Competition among forms of Corporate Governance in the European Community: The Case of Britain', in Berger, S. and Dore, R. (eds) *National Diversity and Global Capitalism*, Ithaca and London, Cornell University Press.

World Bank (1997) *World Development Report*, New York, Oxford University Press.

Yalnizyan, A. (1998) *The Growing Gap*, Toronto, Centre for Social Justice.

Yeatman, A. (1992) 'Women's Citizenship Claims, Labour Market Policy and Globalisation', *Australian Journal of Political Science*, **27**.

Index

Adnett, N., 27
age-related interest groups, 65–8, 71
Albert, M., 8, 11, 85
American Association for Retired
    Persons (AARP), 66
Americans for Generational Equity
    (AGE), 68
Anglo-Saxon capitalism, 7–8, 61, 113–
    14
    see also neoliberalism
Appelbaum, E., 26
attitudes to welfare, 57–9
Australia, 44, 51, 92
Austria, 20

Baker, M., 63
banking sector, 87, 88
Barlow, M., 8, 38–9, 48–9, 56, 59
Barnet, R.J., 27, 44
Barrett, E.J., 58
Bashevkin, S., 65
benefit programmes, 46–7, 77–8, 83–4
Bensaid, D., 69
Bernstein, J., 26
Beveridge plan, 18
Bienenfeld, M., 108
Bilder, B., 125
Binstock, R.H., 67
bond rating agencies, 38–9
Brecher, J., 8
Bretton Woods system, 5
Brodie, J., 64
Bruce, M., 19
Buergenthal, T., 125
Bundesbank, 85

Campbell, B., 38–9, 48–9, 56, 59
Canada, 45, 56, 61
    'creditwatch', 38–9
    interest groups, 65, 66, 68
    NAFTA, 13–14, 27, 127

protests, 69
    social policy, 47, 48–9, 51
Canada Assistance Plan, 48–9
capital
    balance of power shifted towards, 12,
        15, 75–6, 80, 100–1
    exit option, 6, 80
capital controls, 5
capitalism
    collapse of socialist alternative, 1–3
    forms of, 8, 112–14
Castells, M., 88
Castles, F.G., 28, 53, 102
Charnovitz, S., 127
Chretien, Prime Minister, 49
citizenship
    erosion of social citizenship, 45–51
    social standards and, 116–22
civil rights, 117
Clarke, T., 8
Clasen, J., 83–4
Clinton, W., 63, 67
commodification, 8–9
community, 118–19, 120–1
    national community, 15–16, 105–9,
        115–16
company-based welfare, 26–7, 28, 85
competitiveness, international, 7
Confalonieri, M.A., 58
confidence, investor, 39
contingent labour force, 25–7, 31–2
convergence criteria, 13, 40, 84, 98, 128
Cook, F.L., 58
Cornia, G.A., 124
corporate taxes, 41, 43
corporatism, 20, 59–60, 75, 104–5
Costello, T., 8
creditworthiness, 38–9
crises, economic, 38–9, 75, 107
Czerny, P.G., 14

Day, C.L., 65, 66
Deacon, B., 8, 124, 127, 128, 130
debts, national, 15, 37–40, 97–9
deficits, budget, 15, 37–40, 84, 97–9
de-industrialization, 25
democratic deficit, 121
democratic politics *see* national politics
deregulation, 8–10
Dicken, P., 44
Dole, G., 63
Dominelli, L., 62, 63
downsizing the social state, 37–40
Doyal, L., 118–19
Drohan, M., 44, 45
du Rivage, V.L., 26–7
dumping, social, 7, 15, 27–8, 95–7

Earned Income Tax Credit, 50, 51
East Asian capitalism, 114
economic classification of countries, 119–20
economic crises, 38–9, 75, 107
economic growth, 15, 23–4, 33, 94–5
economic IGOs, 122–4, 130
Economic and Monetary Union (EMU), 40, 84, 98
education and training, 22–3
employee benefits, 26–7, 28, 85
employer obligation/responsibility, 28
    see also capital
employment, 15, 18–35
    see also full employment; labour market; unemployment
end of ideology, 6, 102–5
Esping-Andersen, G., 74, 78, 79–80, 81, 103, 116, 117
European model of capitalism, 8, 32, 61, 113–14
European Union (EU), 13, 27, 40, 100
    EMU, 40, 84, 98
    Maastricht Treaty, 13, 40, 84, 98, 128
    Social Charter, 61, 127–8
    social policy, 122, 126–9
exchange rates, 5

feminist movement, 61–5, 71
Field, F., 48
fiscal policy, 41–4
flexibility, labour market, 9, 15, 21–2, 26, 76–7, 81–2, 95–7

Fordism, 24–5
foreign investment, 44–5, 83, 85
France, 6, 20, 40, 56, 65
    Jospin government, 69, 103
Fukuyama, F., 112
Fulcher, J., 77
full employment, 2, 15, 94–5
    end of, 18–20, 75, 90
    Japan, 19, 20, 85, 87, 90

Garrett, G., 17, 104–5
Gelb, J., 63–4
George, V., 55, 58
German Employers' Organization, 85
Germany, 45, 69, 74, 80–5, 90–2
    income distribution and taxation, 82–3
    social protection, 83–4
gerontocratic dominance thesis, 65–8
Gifford, C.G., 65, 66
Ginn, J., 66, 67, 68
Glasman, M., 85
global civil society, 131
global social policy, 111–32
    supranational action on social policy, 122–9
globalization, 3–11
    and the return of unemployment, 20–4
    and role of the state in social protection, 33–4, 99
    social policy and the 'logic' of, 15–16, 94–110
    and social standards, 115–16
Gonyea, J., 63
Goodman, R., 86, 89
Gough, I., 118–19
Gould, A., 78, 79, 83–4, 86
government/state, 5–7
    changing balance of power with capital and labour, 15, 100–1
    globalization and state role in social protection, 33–4, 99
    impact of globalization on policy options, 15, 102–5
    public opinion and government welfare provision, 57–8
Gray, G., 59
Greider, W., 87
growth, economic, 15, 23–4, 33, 94–5

Hall, P.A., 6
Hansson, G., 126
Harding, P., 112
health care, 47, 65, 67
health care insurance, 26–7
Heller, H., 69
Hirst, P., 4, 104
Hooyman, N., 63
Horsman, M., 12
Huber, E., 60, 79
human rights, 122–3, 124–6
Huseby, B.M., 57
Hutton, W., 8

ideology, end of, 6, 102–5
incentives, investment, 45
income distribution
    Germany, 82–3
    growing inequality, 15, 29–32, 95–7
    Japan, 88
    Sweden, 77
income taxes, 41, 42
indirect taxes, 42
industrialized countries, 119–20
inequality, 15, 29–32, 95–7
    legitimization by globalization, 15,
        99–100
inflation, 19–20
institutional conception of state welfare,
    116
interest groups, 59–69, 70–2
intergenerational equity, 67–8
intergovernmental organizations (IGOs),
    122–6, 130–1
international competitiveness, 7
International Covenant on Economic,
    Social and Cultural Rights
    (ICESCR), 125
International Labour Organisation
    (ILO), 95–6, 119, 122, 124–6, 129
International Monetary Fund (IMF), 8–
    9, 39–40, 98, 105, 122
    residual approach to social policy,
        123–4, 130
internationalization, 4
investment, foreign, 44–5, 83, 85
investment incentives, 45
investor confidence, 39
irreversibility of the welfare state, 80

Japan, 7, 14, 32, 74, 85–9, 90–2
    full employment, 19, 20, 85, 87, 90
    globalization, 87–9
job insecurity, 25–7, 31–2
'jobless growth', 23–4
Johnson, N., 48
Jospin, L., 69, 103

Kavanagh, J., 27, 44
Kelsey, J., 10
Kester, W.C., 87
Keynesian Welfare State (KWS), 18
'Keynesianism in one country', 15, 94–5
Kohl, H., 84
Korea, 14

labour
    balance of power shifted away from,
        15, 100–1
    locked into nation state, 115–16
    organized labour, 6, 59–61, 70–1,
        126–7
labour market, 15, 18–35, 90
    changing, 24–7
    flexibility, 9, 15, 21–2, 26, 76–7, 81–
        2, 95–7
    Germany, 81–2
    growing economic inequality and
        social polarization, 29–32
    Japan, 88
    social dumping, 27–8
    Sweden, 19, 20, 75, 76–7
    see also employment; unemployment
laissez-faire capitalism, 2, 112–13
Larkin, J., 62
'lean' production, 25–6
left-of-centre approaches, 15, 54–7,
    102–5
legitimation problem, 2, 3
Leibfried, S., 14
less-developed countries, 120
'lifetime employment', 85, 87
long-term care scheme, 83

Maastricht Treaty, 13, 40, 84, 98, 128
manufacturing, 25
Marshall, A., 12
Marshall, T.H., 116, 118
Martin, A., 11
Martin, H.P., 82

Massey, P., 10
McCarthy, S., 45
McDonald, L., 68
McLaughlin, E., 22
McMurphy, S., 75, 78
McQuaig, L., 104
medical care, 47, 65, 67
Mexico, 13–14, 27
Miller, S., 56
Milner, M., 66
minimum standards, 117
Mishel, L., 26, 30–1
Mishra, R., 2, 3, 20, 54
MNCs: avoidance of tax, 44–5
monetarism, 37
Morley, M., 47
Multilateral Agreement on Investments
    (MAI), 8, 105, 131
Multinational Agreement on Social
    Standards (MASS), 131
Myles, J., 49

NAFTA, 13–14, 27, 122, 126–9
nation state
    decentring, 11–15
    social policy and 'logic' of globaliza-
        tion, 15–16, 105–9
National Action Committee on the
    Status of Women (NAC), 65
national communities, 15–16, 105–9,
    115–16
National Council of Senior Citizens
    (NCSC), 66
national governments *see* government/
    state
national minimum standard of living,
    15, 99–100
national politics, 15–16, 53–73
    'end of ideology' and policy options,
        15, 102–5
    interest groups and social movements,
        59–69
    'logic' of globalization in conflict
        with democratic politics, 15–16,
        105–9
    party competition and social policy,
        54–7
    public opinion and attitudes to
        welfare, 57–9
national solidarity, 15, 99–100

neoliberalism, 2–3, 113–15
    downsizing the social state, 37–40
    fiscal policy, 41
    and globalization, 7–11
    growing economic inequality and
        social polarization, 29–32
Netherlands, 66
New Zealand, 10, 32, 39, 51, 92
    proportional representation, 56–7
    social policy, 48
Newton, K., 58
North American Agreement on Labour
    Co-operation, 127
Norway, 101, 105

occupational benefits, 26–7, 28, 85
O'Connor, J., 62
OECD, 8–11, 39–40, 83, 98, 121
    'Jobs Study', 9–10, 22
    residual approach to social policy,
        122, 124
Olsen, G.M., 76, 77
Olsson, S.E., 75, 78
O'Neill, E., 62
openness, 4–5
organized labour, 6, 59–61, 70–1, 126–7
Orr, A., 10
Osberg, L., 22
Otting, A. 126
Owens, J., 41, 83, 91

partnership, social, 15, 81–2, 100–1
party politics, 15, 53, 54–7, 69–70, 102–
    5
Peele, G., 28
Peng, I., 86, 89
pensions, 65, 67, 68, 78
Perot, R., 56
Petras, J., 47
Pierson, C., 102
Pierson, P., 3, 14, 49, 50, 70
Piven, F.F., 7
Plant, R., 118
pluralism, welfare, 33, 98–9
polarization, social, 29–32
political parties, 15, 53, 54–7, 69–70,
    102–5
political rights, 117
politics *see* national politics
Pontusson, J., 6

poverty, 31
privatization, 8–10
progressive taxation, 30, 58
proportional representation, 56–7
protest movements, 61, 68–9, 70–1
public opinion, 57–9, 70

Reagan, R., 66, 67
recession, 86
reflationary policies, 15, 94–5
regional economic associations, 13–14
    and social policy, 122–3, 126–9
regressive taxation, 29–30, 41–4
regulation, 108–9
    see also social standards
Reich, R., 30, 44, 45
residual approach to social policy, 123–4
retrenching social security, 46–51
revenue, lost, 44–5
Rhodes, M., 128
Rifkin, J., 23, 31
rights, social, 116–22
Ross, G., 128
Ryan, B., 64

SAF, 75
Sainsbury, D., 62
Sandford, C., 41, 43, 83
Scandinavian welfare states, 112
    see also Sweden
Schumann, H., 82
selectivity, 46–51
Silvia, S.J., 61
Singh, A., 127
Skandia, 75
social assistance, 47, 49, 78–9
Social Charter, 61, 127–8
social citizenship *see* citizenship
social clauses, 126–7
social deficit, 121
social dumping, 7, 15, 27–8, 95–7
social expenditure, 15, 36–52, 97–9
    downsizing the social state, 37–40
    eroding social citizenship, 45–51
    fiscal policy, 41–4
    Japan, 85–6
    shrinking tax base, 44–5
social/humanitarian IGOs, 122–3, 124–6, 130
social insurance, 78, 83

social-market capitalism, 8, 32, 61, 113–14
social movements, 59–69, 70–1
social partnership, 15, 81–2, 100–1
social polarization, 29–32
social policy
    after socialism, 111–15
    global, 111–32
    as human rights, 125–6
    and the 'logic' of globalization, 15–16, 94–110
    options constrained by globalization, 15, 102–5
    residual approach, 123–4
    supranational action on, 122–9
    trading regimes and, 126–9
social programmes to assist women, 62–3
social protection, 36–52, 91–2
    downsizing the social state, 37–40
    eroding social citizenship, 45–51
    fiscal policy, 41–4
    Germany, 83–4
    globalization exerts a downward pressure on, 15, 97–9
    globalization weakens ideological underpinning, 15, 99–100
    Japan, 85–6, 87, 88–9
    shrinking tax base, 44–5
    Sweden, 77–9
social rights, 116–22
social security, retrenching, 46–51
Social Security (Minimum Standards) Convention, 126
social standards, 115–31
    globalization and, 115–16
    from social rights to, 116–22
    supranational activity, 122–9
socialism
    collapse of socialist alternative, 1–3
    social policy after, 111–15
standards, social *see* social standards
Stanford, J., 127
state *see* government/state
Stephens, J.D., 53, 60, 76, 79
Streeck, W., 40
structural adjustment programs, 123–4
subsidiarity, 128
substantive rights, 117
Sullivan, K., 91

supranational action on social policy,
122–9
Swardson, A., 49
Sweden, 2, 6, 74, 75–80, 90–2, 112
labour market, 19, 20, 75, 76–7
social protection, 77–9
taxation and income distribution, 77
wage solidarity, 76–7
Swepston, L., 126

taxation, 15, 29–30, 37–8, 90–1, 97–9,
121
fiscal policy, 41–4
Germany, 45, 82–3
public opinion and attitudes to
welfare, 57–9
shrinking tax base, 44–5
Sweden, 77
Taylor-Gooby, P., 46, 58
Teeple, G., 6, 113
Tester, F.J., 124
Therborn, G., 2
third parties, turn to, 56
'third way', 71
Thompson, G., 4, 104
Thurow, L.C., 67–8, 87
Timmins, N., 58
trade, 4–5, 44, 87
trading regimes, 13–14, 122–3, 126–
9
trade unions, 6, 59–61, 70–1, 126–7
training and education, 22–3
Tran, M., 66
transfer pricing, 44
Traynor, I., 69
trickle down, 33
tripartism, 5, 100–1

unemployment, 19–20
Germany, 80–1
globalization and the return of, 20–4
Japan, 86

Sweden, 75
unemployment insurance, 18–19, 46–7,
77–8
United Kingdom (UK), 25, 56
economic inequality, 31–2
labour market, 21–2
older people, 66, 67
social policy, 47–8, 51
United Nations (UN), 119, 122, 124–6,
129
United States (US), 5, 12, 56
de-industrialization, 25
dominant global influence, 11, 124
economic inequality, 30–1
interest groups, 65–6, 67–8
labour market flexibility, 9, 21, 26
NAFTA, 13, 27, 61
organized labour, 61, 126–7
social policy, 47, 49, 50, 51
taxation, 44–5
universality, 46–51

Vinocur, J., 82
voting patterns, 56–7, 63, 67

wages, 15, 20, 25, 26, 95–7
solidarity in Sweden, 76–7
Wallenberg, P., 76
Weir, A., 64
welfare capitalism, 2, 112
welfare pluralism, 33, 98–9
Wilks, S., 76
Williams, F., 64
Wilson, E., 64
withholding tax, 45, 83
workfare, 47, 78
World Bank (WB), 8, 119–20, 122, 123–
4, 130
World Trade Organization (WTO), 8,
105, 106, 122, 126–9

Yeatman, A., 64